THE BEST OF TRAVE

The best of
Travellers' Tales

JEFF WATSON
with PAMELA WRIGHT
Illustrated by Guy Hayes

To Lindsay with love
from Jeff Watson

November 1988

UNWIN PAPERBACKS
Sydney   London   Boston

First published in Australia
by Unwin Paperbacks 1986
Third impression 1987

This book is copyright under the Berne Convention. No
reproduction without permission. All rights reserved.

UNWIN® PAPERBACKS
Allen & Unwin Australia Pty Ltd
8 Napier Street, North Sydney NSW 2060

and Unwin Paperbacks
Park Lane, Hemel Hempstead, Herts HP2 4TE England

© Jeff Watson and Pamela Wright 1986

National Library of Australia
Cataloguing-in-Publication entry:

Watson, Jeff.
The best of Travellers' tales.

ISBN 0 86861 961 2.

1. Voyages and travels—1951— —Anecdotes,
facetiae, satire, etc. I. Wright, Pamela. II. Hayes, Guy.
III. Title. IV. Title: Travellers' tales (Radio program).
910.4

Set in 10.5/11.5pt Baskerville by Setrite Typesetters,
Hong Kong
Printed in Hong Kong by Wing King Tong Co. Ltd.

Contents

Introduction

'TRAVELLERS' Tales' is now in its fifth year, and heard in all the capital cities of Australia. How did it start? Pamela decided to do a radio travel programme and asked Jeff to present it at an audition. For some years Jeff was one of the reporters on the ABC's 'Holiday' programme and travelled the world at vast expense picking to pieces other people's package holidays. The ABC very quickly found that travel agents and airlines were quite prepared to pay for our trips so long as we featured the destination on our programme. What we said was up to us. The end result was a sort of consumer travelogue. Many people watched the programme in the same way that others leaf through coloured brochures in travel agents. They didn't necessarily want to go to the places we featured, or could even afford to, but they had surrogate holidays through the images of pure escapism which we presented.

As working journalists of course we were envied and despised by the rest of the ABC. What a lurk. Life became an endless freeby, and yet we became blasé about the endless jet-setting. Holidays, which should be looked forward to and even earned, became an endless chore. What was it that George Bernard Shaw said: 'A perpetual holiday is a good working definition of hell.'

'Holiday' became what the ABC chose to call 'an information programme.' It had the two basic requirements of any television programme—colour and movement. It was moderately informative, if bland. The problem which vexed us all was how critical should we be? Would we be failing in our duty if we didn't mention that our breakfast egg was not soft, but hard-boiled? If it rained, was that the travel agent's fault? Would we write off an entire holiday simply because we encountered one surly cab driver?

In the final analysis, as the Americans say, it didn't really matter whether we were critical or not. We might carp about the freezing air conditioning or the warm beer, but the vast majority of our fellow holidaymakers had paid their money and they were going to enjoy themselves even if it killed them. Sometimes it did.

During one particularly awful outback bus tour, the little old pensioner lady who clung defiantly to her handbag, gritted her teeth and said: 'I've saved all year for this trip, and I'm damned if I'm not going to enjoy it.'

Of all the 'Holiday' programmes made, very few captured those humorous little vignettes that make it all seem worthwhile. The camera cannot lie but film costs money, so we were frequently trying to recapture something genuinely funny that had already happened. So it was about this time that we got together to start 'Travellers' Tales.' It was just the right outlet for the well told tale, the travel story that told more about a country than anything you could read in the world atlas.

A great many tourists these days collect tourist attractions like others select their groceries in the supermarket: the Eiffel Tower, the Pyramids, the Taj Mahal, the Golden Gate Bridge. What 'Travellers' Tales' is interested in is not so much the sights themselves, but how travellers react to them.

Noël Coward, that great traveller, always maintained that although he had gazed upon many of the world's wonders, he could not recall a single detail of them in his mind's eye. It mattered little to him which way the Tower of Pisa leaned. The pleasure in travelling, for Coward, was the joy of departure and the anticipation of arriving. There was never a sight for Coward that didn't look better looking back.

Travel is about places, but more importantly it is about people. The stories in this book are about both.

Australians are inveterate travellers. Although they are perhaps not quite so visible as the Americans, the Japanese or the Germans, even so they have an extraordinary knack of getting into the most remote places. This, of course, has a lot to do with the remoteness of the continent, and the fact that six hours after leaving Sydney airport in a Jumbo jet, you are still flying over Australia. When Australians go away they have to go a long way to get anywhere, which costs a lot of money. So when they go, for example to Europe, there are no restrictions. A grand European tour is a grand European tour—everywhere from Athens to Amsterdam and then more.

The international Australian has the habit of appearing in the most bizarre places. Patrick Cook, the cartoonist, tells the story of a holiday in Jerusalem when a friend took him diving under the water in a public swimming pool. At the bottom of the pool there was an entrance to a tunnel which led under the ancient city. Half way through the tunnel, which could scarcely

have been regarded as a public thoroughfare, they met a man trying to light a paraffin lamp. 'Excuse me, mate,' said the man in the broadest Strine. 'You don't know how to light one of these bastards, do you?'

Australians have obviously made their mark on countries of the Third World. A camel driver at the Pyramids in Egypt proudly showed me the scars on his arms caused in a scrap with an Australian tourist. 'Australians,' he said ruefully, 'are very good fighters.'

At Alexandria, also in Egypt, the locals still talk nostalgically about the night the Australian 7th Division burned down the local cinema because they objected to the film being shown.

At Cape Canaveral in Florida there is a fish restaurant called Fisherman's Wharf. It's speciality is catfish, not just to be eaten but to be observed. The restaurant is on a wooden pier which juts out into the bayou (Australians would call it a swamp). In the centre of the restaurant is a hole in the boards. A light is placed near the hold to attract the catfish. The waitresses still remember the night an Australian tourist took off all his clothes and dived into the hole, only to emerge with hundreds of small fish hanging on to him.

Australians are still the best customers at the Munich Beer Festival, and it was there that I heard the most classic one-liner ever uttered by an Australian ex-pat. Calling the waiter over, he said in a loud voice, 'I'd like a drink.' '*Bitte, mein Herr*,' said the waiter. 'No thanks,' said the Australian, 'I'll have a Scotch.'

American plastic

THEY have an expression in America to sum up everything that is synthetic, second-rate and awful—American Plastic. Nowhere is that expression more appropriate than when applied to American motels. From Maine to Albuquerque (or possibly from Mechanicsburg, Virginia to Boise, Idaho) they are consistent in their awfulness. The walls are thin, the carpet is nylon, the bathroom cabinet is made of vinyl-covered laminated chipboard, and the loo has a small strip of paper across it telling you it has been sanitised. On the washbasin are two tumblers wrapped in plastic which have also been sanitised for your convenience. It is so convenient in fact that it is usually impossible to remove the wrappings.

Attached to the bed, if you are very lucky, is a coin box. If you insert a quarter, the whole bed vibrates up and down like a breathless water buffalo. Of course, the Americans invented motels, and we all know what people are supposed to do in them, but surely not in a bed like *that*?

One of the best examples of American Plastic motels is to be found in Hanford, California. It is called the Hanford Motor Lodge, and it is the only place in town. If the owners feel like sueing, I don't care, because it is AWFUL.

You would have to be fairly odd to be in Hanford in the first place. It's one of those towns in between San Francisco and Los Angeles, on Route 101. If you blinked you would probably miss

it, and if you did you would be extremely fortunate. In addition to being the world's most boring town, Hanford also boasts the world's most extraordinary moteliers (if that is what they call people who run motels). Many Americans are blissfully unaware of any other country except their own. If a visitor is not American, then he must be Canadian. Americans are conditioned to Canadians because the biggest tourist migration in the world is from Canada to America and vice versa. It is no good at all telling people about Sydney being in Australia, because you will find they've written you down as SIDNEY (sic) BC (British Columbia) in the register.

The lady who ran the Hanford Motor Lodge was no exception. She would have passed for Shelley Winters in *Come Back Little Sheba*. The earth mother type, complete with a 1950s hairstyle and a cleavage through which you could have driven a Mack truck. From the corner of her mouth drooped a permanent cigarette.

I kept thinking, no wonder Norman Bates killed his mother. Shelley spoke: 'If you're only stayin' one night that'll be twenty-two fifty in advance.'

Had she, I enquired, ever been to Australia? 'No honey, I ain't ever been out of the State, but I hear it's real beautiful over there.' She waved an arm. 'Over there' meant vaguely in the direction of the all-nite diner on the other side of the road.

Next to the diner was the only bar in town. We entered through the bead curtain. Two men in cowboy hats looked up from their beers. Kenny Rogers on the jukebox. At the bar, the town hooker, 40 in the shade, gazed on us with a smile like an insanitary crocodile. 'Good afternoon, Gennlmun,' she breathed. 'Ah you by any chance from the U-nited King-dom?' No, we protested, we were typewriter salesmen from Australia. The voice became more conspiratorial. 'Lemme give you a word of advice,' she said. 'This town is full of weirdos and wet-backs. Keep your hand on your money and look out for Mexicans with switchblades.'

While we considered this statement, she went on, 'Do you realise, I am the local Avon representative, and ah got 50 girls workin' under me.'

'Madam,' said my companion, 'I'm not a bit surprised.'

We retreated in confusion to the Hanford Motor Lodge. Were there, we enquired of Norman Bates' mother, any calls? 'Oh yeah,' said Shelley, 'we had some guy from Switzerland call you.'

'But we don't know anybody in Switzerland,' I protested. 'Where was the call from? Lucerne, Geneva, Zurich?'

Shelley removed her cigarette, 'Oh gee, I don't know. Some place called Sid-ney. Sid-ney, Switzerland.' Again the arm flapped in the direction of the diner. I guess if you follow the road from the diner sooner or later it will take you anywhere *Over There*.

Tai Chi

I can still visualise this elderly Chinese man walking along the waterfront in Shanghai with two steel balls on his head. It was six in the morning and it was my last chance to watch the Chinese performing tai-chi. Since 1959 this form of mental and physical exercise has become an obsession with the population of China. The movements of the most popular form of tai-chi are slow and graceful (there's also boxing tai-chi for the fast mover) and on this morning there were at least a thousand enthusiasts bending and twisting to the music in their grey or blue Mao suits. A rather distorted tune emanated from a loud speaker strung up in a tree and, for as far as the sound reached along the waterfront, tai-chi devotees were putting their hearts and souls into this activity. Meanwhile, the barges and cargo ships were blasting their horns and China's busiest harbour was awash with activity. Surprisingly this added to, rather than detracted from, the serenity of the intense tai-chi performers.

I had managed to persuade some travelling companions to rise before dawn and accompany me on a tai-chi-watching spree. It was quite mesmerising to stare at people involved in this early morning sport but the most surprising spectacle was a man surrounded by hundreds of onlookers. At first we didn't take a great deal of notice as the Chinese create crowds at any vaguely unusual occurrence. But the crowd was expanding rapidly so this obviously was something extraordinary.

Here was a man performing what we were told was an ancient form of kung fu. He was balancing two enormous steel balls, each 6 inches in diameter, on his head. Expressionless, he began moving slowly towards Huangpu Park, punching the air with vigorous, aggressive movements. He continued to walk right through the hundreds of Chinese still performing tai-chi with every inch of concentration. Not one of them blinked an eyelid as he balanced his balls and his fists missed their faces by inches. Which proves, I guess, that tai-chi is incredibly relaxing.

A ball in the hand is worth two on the head. I still wonder if it was ancient kung fu or is it true that there's always one in every crowd?

The Legion's last patrol

'EXCUSE me, whack, could you pass the peanuts, *s'il vous plait?*' I was sitting at the bar of the Maeva Beach Hotel in Tahiti and it was a long time since anyone had called me 'whack'. It clearly identified the man with the military crewcut as coming from Liverpool, England. On the dance-floor, a number of overweight Americans were being persuaded to dance the hula by a girl in a grass skirt. What sort of man was it, I speculated, who would speak French with a Liverpool accent?

'I'm in the Foreign Legion,' he continued. 'You know, with the Frogs. We're guarding *le bombe atomique*. In Mururoa.'

Earlier that day, at the airport, I had seen a French Airforce Caravelle disgorging soldiers. This was one of them, and he was on R & R. 'We sit around in huts playing cards, bored stiff,' he said warming to his subject. 'Then we feel something go "whumph" underground. There's another one gone, we say.'

What on earth was an Englishman doing in the *Force de Frappe?* 'I was in Argyll and Sutherland Highlanders. And the Black Watch. Bloody good regiments. But the British Army's gone soft. And Britain has. Look at the way they've given Africa back to a pack of bloody niggers.' I could see it was going to be one of those conversations. The man with the Liverpool accent said his name was Jack. He was stocky and muscular and looked very fit. A tough customer.

10

His story was like something out of a Beau Geste adventure. He had left home after a row with his wife, hitchhiked to one of the Channel Ports and caught a boat to France. There, he'd enlisted in the Legionnaires. He'd toured all the world's trouble spots...Africa, Algeria, Guyana. Mururoa Atoll was the cushiest posting he'd ever had. But he was bored. Slapping his belly with a ham-sized fist he said: 'I'm going soft. I'm a professional soldier. I'm trained to kill. I know how to trim the wick on a hand grenade so that it goes off in four seconds, not eight. Do you want me to show you how to do it?'

I said I was an office worker and didn't have much use for hand grenades. Meanwhile Jack was getting drunker and drunker and more expansive with gestures. I thought it was probably time to go. Suddenly he threw his arm around my shoulders and said: 'Tell me, what's it like in England now? You've been there recently haven't you? What's it like?'

Since running away from home Jack hadn't been back to the land of his birth in fifteen years. And then quite suddenly, he burst into tears. 'I have a son there but I've never seen him. My wife said I could never see him even if I did go back.'

Breathing heavily, Jack stumbled off to his room. On the dance floor a man from Minnesota in plaid trousers was still having difficulty grasping the hula.

What was it somebody said about some corner of a foreign field that is forever England? I've often wondered if Jack found it.

Making friends for Australia

Hotels in the Soviet Union would probably not find their way to the top of the list of the world's most luxurious. The service is usually poor by Western standards, the room service non-existent, the plumbing a nightmare, the food stodgy and unimaginative. Guests are often told to be their own bath plugs, because they are almost completely unobtainable in the Soviet

Union and those which are supplied are usually stolen.

Picture, if you can, the arrival of an Australian television crew in Moscow. They had come to film the Moscow Olympics. Already they had suffered the indignity of having to carry their own baggage to their rooms on the first floor. Together they surveyed their bleak little rooms. A single bed, a tattered blind and a threadbare carpet. A bedside lamp that didn't work. A cracked washstand. And no bath plug.

The sound recordist, being of a suspicious nature, was convinced that the room was bugged. He searched in vain for hidden microphones—behind the pictures, underneath the telephone, beneath the bed. There was only one other conceivable location: the threadbare rug in the centre of the floor. Pulling it back he revealed a small brass plate in the centre of the floor, secured with four nuts. Taking a spanner from his tool kit (sound recordists always come prepared, like Boy Scouts), he removed the four nuts, but nothing happened. Perplexed, he replaced the rug.

Half an hour later, one of the team went down to the lobby to find 50 Russians gazing bemusedly upon a chandelier which had fallen from the ceiling.

The real thing

THE QE2 is a ship that most of us would give our right arm to travel on. But the prices are fairly restrictive unless you happen to be rich and famous. Wilton Morley and his actor father, Robert, are undoubtedly both, but in Miami, USA, they boarded as first class guests of the shipping line to film a *QE2* promotion before reaching the Papa Doc country of Haiti. Robert, obviously used to the best, was content with first class accommodation until he discovered that there was the even more glamourous Executive Class. So, in between takes of the commercial they were making, he exerted all his energy trying to arrange admission into the Executive Class dining room only to be turned away. As son Wilton said with a smile, 'Something he didn't care for at all.'

Eventually they arrived at Haiti and Robert and Wilton were the only passengers to disembark. Understandably it is not regarded as the perfect holiday island by either the English or the Americans, and these solitary travellers were met on the quay by a less than savoury Haitian character. It was six in the morning, and this 'Graham Greene' eccentric had donned a straw hat, was carrying a cane stick and bowed and scraped to the famous Robert Morley as they made their way to the hotel.

The only other guests of any note were Vincent Price and his wife, Coral Browne. As king of horror films, Vincent was exceedingly keen to attend a voodoo ceremony, and was advised of a show in Haiti's impoverished capital of Port-au-Prince. The black magic ritual is open to any tourists who can be persuaded to attend.

The scene was set and the chanting had just begun when the intrepid four arrived. These distinguished visitors were greeted by a roll of drums, a courtesy to which they were expected to reply by offering a few gourdes (the local coins). In that evening's voodoo ceremony, the gods were offered a chicken (sometimes it's a goat, pig or bull). Before immolating this chicken, its wings and legs were broken and death was inflicted by pulling its head off with a quick, twisting movement. To add further to the gore, the victim's windpipe was ripped out by the sacrificer's teeth and the offering was made to the gods. Burning candles encircled a sandy patch among the trees and Wilton confirmed, 'The scene was rather eerie with the locals chanting and wailing and swirling like zombies. I think I heard a semblance of a wail from Vincent, too.'

Laughing about the evening, Wilton recalled, 'We were all right, but poor old Vincent became quite ill. I suppose all those years of tomato ketchup in those horror films hadn't prepared him for the real thing!'

Not a rat, Mr Fawlty

FIVE hundred kilometres is a long way to drive when your only companion is a grinning Indian driver and Elvis Presley's Greatest Hits. We were in Malaysia, driving from Singapore to the Genting Highlands along the suicidal coast road. Every five miles or so there was an accident. The side of the road was littered with burnt-out cars and I was more than glad not to be driving. Our driver, Ahmed, was barely coping with the traffic conditions, and he clung to the kerb like a leech. We had probably not exceeded 30 miles an hour since leaving Singapore. The road signs exhorted us in Tamil and English to drive safely: 'Better five minutes late in this world than twenty-five years too early in the next.'

'Overtaker = Undertaker'

'Leave Your Blood at the Bloodbank, Not on the Highway.'

As for Elvis, he was on the bench seat between us. Ahmed only had one cassette. It included 'All Shook Up', 'Hound Dog', 'Jailhouse Rock' and 'Don't Be Cruel'. When Ahmed had played it through, he turned it over and played the other side. Every time I awoke after a doze it was to the sound of The King going: 'Uh-huh-huh'. 'Very good music, sah,' said Ahmed, his teeth flashing in the tropical gloom.

That part of Malaysia probably wouldn't rate as one of the world's great scenic drives. With endless rubber plantations, it is a kind of luxuriant green hell which blots out the sun. On the side of the road, the occasional fruit stall sold durian—that pineapple–shaped fruit which smells like sweaty socks and has to be eaten with a clothes peg on the nose. Ahmed grinned: 'Tastes like heaven, smells like hell,' he said, as if he had just invented the saying.

Late in the afternoon, the road started to wind uphill into the Genting Highlands and the scenery started to get interesting. There were waterfalls and tropical orchids; monkeys peeped out from among the leaves and large tropical butterflies flitted about. This was more like it.

At the top of the hill stood the Genting Highlands hotel complex. It was difficult to see how anyone could have designed something so hideous in such a beautiful natural setting; a monstrous slab of reinforced concrete perched on the side of a cliff. In the centre of it was an artificial lake, the centrepiece of which was a concrete grotto with grotesque concrete animals. A few dejected Malays paddled their new brides around the lake in rowing boats. Apparently this was *the* big honeymoon spot for Kuala Lumpur and Singapore.

It was while we were on the conducted tour that we first saw the dead rats in the swimming pool. There were two. One had died with its feet in the air, but the other must have had all the weight in its behind because its little whiskery head was sticking out above the water.

'Get a shot of the rats,' hissed the director to the cameraman. This was easier said than done. It was by now late afternoon.

The rats were drifting into the dark side of the pool and unfortunately the only way to film them was to prod them out into the sunlit part. I got a stick and prodded them into the sunlight while the hotel manager wasn't looking. This involved walking the narrow strip of concrete at the edge of the swimming pool with a 300−foot drop on the other side. Finally, the dead rats were immortalised on celluloid.

We were after all, a *consumer* travelogue programme. It was our duty to report on vacations and hotels and tell the story as we found it. When the scene of the dead rats in the swimming pool appeared on Australian television, all hell broke loose. The Malaysian Government made it clear that we would, henceforth, be *persona non grata* in Malaysia. For some reason, I can not remember another detail about Malaysia. But I think of the place every time I hear Elvis singing 'All Shook Up'.

The Red Baron

EVERY Sunday afternoon over Sydney harbour, you will see a little red biplane puttering about. It is a de Havilland Tiger Moth made more than 40 years ago, and it is owned by Dave Voight, the Red Baron. Dave Voight's scenic tours represent the best value for money air flips anywhere in the world, and over the world's most beautiful harbour too. You stagger around the sky at a stately 70 miles an hour, stickybeaking into the windows of the skyscrapers and doing aerial wheelies around Centrepoint Tower.

For $50, Dave will take you up the harbour to Manly, then back again. He'll loiter over landmarks like the Opera House and the Bridge so that you can get your shots. And the Tiger Moth is an excellent plane for aerial photography. Wearing your leather Biggles helmet and your Steve McQueen bomber jacket, you can simply lean over the side and snap away.

Until recently, Dave used to operate the Tiger from Kingsford Smith International Airport. The fun part was taxiing out and awaiting clearance for take-off, lined up behind a fat-bottomed Jumbo carrying 350 passengers. For those who are used to jetting around in boring Jumbos, the Tiger represents a whole new flying experience. There are two open cockpits and Dave flies the plane from the rear seat so the passenger is sitting immediately behind an enormous wooden prop. The starting routine is just like those World War I movies: 'Switches on',

'Switches off', 'Contact'. When it's ticking over, the Tiger sounds like an old motor bike. Dave lines it up on Mascot's two-mile-long runway, then it's two bumps and you are airborne. The noise is unbelievable. The slipstream fills up your mouth with air and your cheeks flap like bladders. 'Wurrup-wurrup', goes the motor. The little Tiger Moth goes so slowly that, even with its wheels down, a Jumbo is still going considerably faster.

I do hope the wowsers don't drive Dave Voight out of business. He's a great Australian and a fine pilot, and he offers the travelling public a genuine piece of airborne nostalgia.

At the time of writing, Dave Voight is considering a new venture—fitting out the front passenger cockpit with a small bar so that travellers can mix themselves splits. He is also talking about operating night flights over the harbour. So if you hear drunken laughter coming from above your head and the sound of an old motor bike engine, you'll know who it is...

Anything to declare?

THE worst part about travelling is coming home and having to get through customs. You're tired, unshaven, heavily jet-lagged, and the extra bottle of Chivas Regal you have illicitly secreted into your suitcase might just as well have neon lights attached to it. *And* before you go home for your well-earned shower and kip you have to run the gauntlet of a number of highly alert public servants.

It is very interesting while standing in the customs queue, waiting your turn, to look at the people around you. The layers peel off and we all become single human units; there is a common bond in suffering. How well can we all conceal our guilt? The strange thing is that many people start sweating and going red in the face even if they aren't concealing anything.

Customs officers are a bit like the ancient mariner; they stoppeth one in three. Professional travellers tend to put their heads down as soon as they leave the aircraft and make sure they are at the head of the crew. They try to get a male officer rather than a female one; the ladies tend to be a bit more thorough.

It is not a good idea to make jokes with customs officers. Return their gaze evenly and honestly, be polite and courteous and don't, whatever you do, become hostile. Try to arrange it so that if you have to open your case you can do so with the minimum of fuss. Some people think that customs officers are

fazed by heaps of dirty underwear. Don't you believe it. I once stood next to a man who disguised a number of small antiques by wrapping them up in dirty socks. The customs man wasn't a bit bothered and solemnly peeled them off to reveal the contraband—a plaster cast of Chopin's hand. Another dodge is ladies carrying babes in arms. Now I ask you, if you were a customs officer wouldn't you be suspicious if the baby started bawling its head off just as it reached the end of the queue. Isn't it just as likely that Mum just pinched it?

Everybody is familiar with the standard allowance: a litre of booze, 200 cigarettes and gifts to the value of $200, but in recent years an increasing number of animal products have become no-no's. If you are wearing crocodile skin shoes or carrying a crocodile skin handbag, they will take it off you; the same goes for fur coats if the fur is from an animal not bred on a farm, like mink. Ocelot, leopard or tiger skins are out, being, of course, protected animals. If you pick up sea shells on the beach you can bring them in, but not turtle shells because the turtle is also an endangered species. And on the subject of turtles, I have a friend who once smuggled in a small turtle in her bra. She kept it alive on the long flight from San Franciso by periodically taking it to the loo and letting it splash around in the hand basin. She got it past the customs all right. It was just when Mum gave her a welcoming hug that things got a bit difficult. I'm pleased to report however that Somerset (that's what she called him) did survive.

One of the saddest sights at any international airport is the Greek and Italian mommas trying to bring in sausage from home for son Luigi. You cannot bring in meat of any sort, so all that lovely salami ends up in the incinerator. Conversely, you can take meat to Japan. A side of beef is a much more accept-able gift than a plywood boomerang. If you are a butter freak you can bring in a box of butter from New Zealand so long as it is not in commercial quantities.

But in the long term my advice is: if you have anything to declare, declare at least some of it. Or I could recycle the best one-liner of all time: Oscar Wilde at the New York customs— 'Anything to declare, Mr Wilde?' 'I have nothing to declare, except my genius.'

Sugar-daddy

'SUGAR-DADDY' is a word you hear rarely these days. But I met one once on a round the world air cruise. Kev had so much money he didn't know what to do with it so he treated himself and his diamond-spangled girlfriend, Janine, to this exotic cruise.

The Jumbo seating had been rearranged so that everyone was travelling first class. About eight rows of seats had actually been removed to make room for a well stocked bar that was virtually never closed. This area became headquarters for millionaire Kev and his lady. Most of the passengers on board enjoyed the free—flowing champagne or the Drambuie on ice, but not nearly as much as Kev did. It took schooners of Drambuie to satisfy him and he was so constantly inebriated that he didn't even notice when we swooped low over Easter Island or the exhilarating low-level flight along the spine of the magnificant Andes. At one stage he managed to ask me if I could take a couple of photographs from the window of the plane of 'anything really' I tried to oblige but there were no batteries in Kev's camera although he insisted he had only just loaded it.

There was too much to see and do for any of us to worry greatly about Kev's drinking habits. But by the second day everyone knew that he was a chronic alcoholic and one passenger was heard to say, 'Steer clear of the bloke in the brown suit. He falls all over you.' The doctor had warned Kev to 'lay off or else' on many occasions and, as it became increasingly obvious that he was an incredible nuisance to other passengers, the stewards and stewardesses were asked by Janine not to serve him any more alcohol. That was easier said than done as Kev was well practised and had his own secret supply. In the week it took us to reach Rio de Janeiro, he had consumed more booze than I could imagine anyone else getting through in a month.

Kev died in his hotel room in Rio. He was more than sixty. Janine, in her early thirties, was very blonde, very tall, very elegant and very determined. Of course it *had* been a sugar-daddy arrangement and Janine *was* inordinately fond of Kev and emotionally distraught at his death. So much so that it took two whole days for time to heal this painful wound. However, Janine knew which side her bread was buttered on. There were plenty more eligible but ageing bachelors on board the air cruise and this was obviously a golden opportunity to make a move.

As the jumbo winged its way out of Rio towards Nairobi, you couldn't help but notice what a fine couple Janine and Glen made. And Glen was much more handsome, and much richer than Kev plus he hadn't quite reached the big Six-O. Kenya here we come. Ain't travel wonderful? Especially when you have mountains of money to 'sweeten the experience'.

The rocket man

CAPE Canaveral in Florida always used to sound like the most exciting place to me. When I finally went there it was a big disappointment. A fetid, low-lying swampland full of mosquito-ridden stagnant pools and tired palm trees. The town of Cocoa Beach, itself a run down beach suburb with decaying condominiums, seedy motels and broken down cars. Even the celebrated Miami surf looked uninteresting. Was this the place, I wondered, that flung Neil Armstrong all the way to the moon?

Since the heady days of the Apollo missions, Canaveral has been going through something of a decline. When I first went there, Columbia, the first Space Shuttle, had not yet proven itself and was years behind schedule. The launch pads were deserted and overgrown with weeds. Huge, rusting girders stood about the place like the discarded pieces of a gigantic construction set. It was in this extraordinary, almost extra-terrestrial landscape, that I first clapped eyes on a man called Al Seeschaaf. Al was leading a party of journalists around the Cape and briefing them on the forthcoming Shuttle launch. 'We're gonna put two guys in dat thing,' he said, waving his arms vaguely in the direction of Launch Pad 39A.

Al was a Jewish New Yorker. He had seen every mission from the Cape since the year dot. When Alan Shepherd wet his pants while waiting for the first sub-orbital launch, Al was there. Al was there when Kennedy had stood talking to Werner von

Braun with his hands dug deep into his pockets. Al was there when Grissom, White and Chaffee had burned themselves to death in the capsule fire. Al had seen Cape Canaveral become Cape Kennedy and then revert to Cape Canaveral again because the locals preferred the original Red Indian name.

Al Seeschaff did not look like a public relations man. Unlike the rest of the dull NASA press office, Al was flamboyant and a snappy dresser. On that first day when I saw him, he was dressed in a bright green silk shirt and a pair of crimson Dacron pants. On his fingers were those silver and turquoise rings that tourists buy in southern California. 'He looks like his ass is on fire,' murmured a colleague. 'Why don't they put *him* into orbit?'

But when it came to the space programme at the Cape, Al had a mind like a computer file. 'We ain't never lost a man in space yet,' he said. 'The Russians have lost lots of guys. Maybe 20 guys, who knows.'

Al Seeschaaf always seemed to be acting out some character in the movies. He spoke out of the corner of his mouth like Edward G. Robinson and chain-smoked like Bogart. Usually you would see him herding a sullen bunch of journalists about the place in buses. 'Move em out,' he'd shout. 'Everybody back on de bus.'

I never did get to see the Space Shuttle lift-off. I went to the Cape many times but the launch was always delayed. Every time I did go there, however, Al Seeschaaf always had some time for 'de guys from Down Under'.

Al Seeschaaf lived to see thirteen launches of the Space Shuttle before lung cancer claimed him. His wife and family still live at Cocoa Beach, and the red dacron pants still hang in the closet. When he died in 1983, the Cape lost one of its most colourful figures. Somehow I can't help hearing Al every time I see pictures of the Space Shuttle. 'We're gonna put two guys in dat thing! It ain't ever flown in space before, but we're gonna put two guys in dat thing.'

Tipping

To tip or not to tip; that is the question. And by tipping I mean not suggesting to the cab driver number three in the fourth race at Rosehill, but actually giving him what Graham Greene used to call a dash, a bribe or a small amount of moolah.

Generally, as a race, we are not renowned for being lavish with the Oxfords. For a start most people wouldn't dream of tipping cab drivers and most cabbies wouldn't expect a tip either. There is none of that servant-master relationship typified by British cab drivers. Have you noticed how British cabbies always call you 'Guvnor' or 'Squire', inferring that only guvnors or squires can afford to use cabs and therefore can also afford lavish tips.

I travelled the whole length of Oxford Street in London once being told what a lousy bunch of tippers Australians were. At the end of the journey the cabbie added another pound to the fare. When I asked what it was for, he said, 'Well, I talked to yer, didn't I Guvnor?' Yes, these days, for irrepressible Cockney charm read ratlike cunning.

The Americans are reputedly the world's biggest tippers and I think they have a lot to answer for. The United States Information Service will quite readily provide you with a list of tipping charges in the States. Cab fares require an extra 15−20 per cent; railway conductors a dollar a night; eating out 15−20

29

per cent on top of the bill. But guess what, you don't have to tip airline employees or people who work in self-serve restaurants. What a relief.

When it comes to unloading your bags outside the hotel there are widening circles of rip-offs. Not only are you expected to tip the doorman who unloads the cab, but also the bellhops a minimum of 50 cents a suitcase.

It is even worse in parts of Europe, particularly in France, where they are inclined to add today's date to the bill. In Switzerland, waiters in some of the poshest hotels will even pay to get their jobs, so obviously someone somewhere is tipping well. Usually though, in Europe, it's the 10 per cent *servis compris* which means you pay a tip whether you like it or not.

In Australia, too, it is creeping in. Not long ago, I was charged $2.10 corkage in a BYO Vietnamese restaurant in Canberra and that was for taking in an ordinary wine cask.

Some good places to go where they don't expect a tip? Refreshingly, New Caledonia and Fiji. In New Caledonia the Wallesians don't expect a tip and neither do the cheerful Fijians. Mind you, the Fijians have their own curious idea about fast service. I once asked for a beer, saw the waiter walk to where the band was playing, sit in on guitar and sing a number and only after that did he bring me a drink.

So what to do when you have reached the awful moment when the bellhop has carried your cases to the room and stands there rattling the change in his pocket and you suddenly realise you have nothing smaller than a $50 note. We suggest that you do a John Cleese routine, feign sickness and plunge into the bathroom with your hand over your mouth. But don't forget that when the bellhop calls the doctor, he too will want a tip.

Fear of flying

I T is no secret that more people suffer from fear of flying than they care to admit. Next time you are in a plane and its just revving up to take off, just take a glance at the people around you; they may be nonchalantly leafing through the financial pages but secretly they're crossing their fingers or gripping the armrests until their knuckles go white. It's a dead giveaway.

I well remember my first flight in a leaky Dakota from a grass airfield in Kent in England. It was one of those no frills flights: the hostess looked as if she cracked walnuts with her knees, the floor was festooned with litter and someone had been eating fish and chips in my seat. The pilot came up, put his hand on my shoulder and said, 'First flight is it? That's OK it's mine too.' Pilot's joke.

It is not all that reassuring being asked to visit the flight deck either. For a start, neither the captain nor first officer usually appears to be driving the aircraft; neither of them has their hands on the controls. Last time I went up to the flight deck one of the crew was peeling an orange and the other was having forty winks.

Still, imagine having to drive a Jumbo for a living; thirteen hours of unrelenting boredom with a challenging half hour at the beginning and end of each flight. Why do Jumbo pilots sit so high up? And is anyone really listening when the hosties do that lifejacket and oxygen routine? It's usually delivered with a happy smile and a jolly inflexion. I've always wondered whether the hosties would still be smiling if it were for real. The best aside I ever heard while the emergency routine was being delivered was from a French steward on a UTA flight to Tahiti. You know that bit in the safety drill where they tell you not to inflate your lifejacket until you get out of the plane? Then when you're in the water blow your whistle to attract attention. Under his breath the steward said, '*Les requins*'. . .sharks.

There are people who believe, of course, that the safest seats in the plane are in the back and certainly when you look at many plane crashes it is usually the tail section that survives. Another chap I know insists on getting a seat near the emergency exit and has memorised the operation of the door handle in the event of a crash.

Most accidents, of course, occur during take-off and landing and 60 per cent of those are what the air safety people call survivable. That means you might survive the impact but you probably won't survive the fire that follows. But let's face it, if it happens in mid-air at least it's quick. There probably isn't even time for that final message from the hosties. 'Ladies and gentlemen will you now put your seat in the fully upright position, remove spectacles and dentures, put your head between your knees and kiss your posterior good-bye.'

Two little words

DR David Livingstone discovered Victoria Falls, the mighty waters of the Zambesi River, in 1855. More than twice as wide and twice as deep as Niagara Falls, they span the entire breadth of the river at one of its widest points, nearly 2 kilometres across. Then the falls plunge over a sheer precipice to a maximum depth of 100 metres. Surprisingly, the river doesn't gather speed as it nears the drop and the approach is signalled only by the thunderous roar and characteristic veil of mist. The local Kalolo Lozi tribe named the falls *Mosi oa tunya*—(the smoke that thunders)—and on a clear day, when the river is raging, this mist is even visible from a distance of 50 kilometres. Upon discovering Victoria Falls, Livingstone said: 'Scenes so lovely must have been gazed upon by angels in their flight.' Tourists can walk from one end to the other through a very natural setting; apart from a pathway, there are only a few pebbles at the edge of the chasm and you can look down into what seems like infinity.

Peter Bowers, someone who could perhaps be described as a hardened political journalist, was totally overwhelmed by the spectacle. He exclaimed: 'You've got this lush, jungly, green vegetation and you suddenly come out into the sunlight and you're struck by another blinding rainbow. It's a rainforest in the precise sense of the word. With the mist from the falls, it's raining 24 hours a day. It's all too much for the senses.'

To appreciate its magnificence you *must* walk the entire length but, for an overall view, twin-engined *Piper Aztecs* operate fifteen-minute joy flights, circling the falls four times with a bonus low-level flight. Four of us, plus the pilot, took off on this appropriately named 'Flight of the Angels' and flew towards the cataract. So that everyone could get the best view possible, our pilot tipped the wings from side to side and at one stage he did this so far that one wing was pointing directly at the water. Then the *Piper Aztec* collected speed, the pilot dipped its nose and we virtually dived into the chasm. It took a great deal of concentration to put danger aside and appreciate that we were flying over, or indeed through, one of the greatest natural wonders of the world. It was a dizzying but delightful experience and on touchdown we all felt rather queasy. Still, Peter managed to sum it all up with: 'If there are two words for coming to Africa, and if there are two words for coming to Zimbabwe, then I'll say them—Victoria Falls.'

Airports—worst in the world

IT's a sad fact these days that travel, which should be romantic and glamorous, begins and ends for most people in airports which are neither. Airports are both indispensable and unbearable. They hold you in limbo—*not yet* having departed and *not yet* having arrived. Unfortunately, we all need them.

In the course of travelling I guess I've passed through about 100 or more airports and they all seem to give you one thing— airport catalepsy. The symptoms are a death-like stupor, a total emptying of the head and a need to be led around by the hand. If you look around Mascot or Tullamarine when the early morning flights come in, everybody seems to be suffering from it.

People with airport catalepsy don't respond to announcements over the public address system, usually because they can't understand a word. I once sat next to a lady with a Dubrovnik boarding pass in her hand who sat oblivious while they called her flight for the third and final time. 'Excuse me,' I said, 'aren't you going to Dubrovnik?' 'No,' she said, 'I'm going to Yugoslavia.'

Airports anywhere have the ability to turn the most mild mannered and inoffensive people into raving loonies. And the more people tell me how big, modern and efficient airports are, the more my lip is inclined to curl. Oh yes, I've seen Charles de Gaulle airport in Paris, where passengers travel along conveyor belts inside perspex tubes. But if the place is so super why were people fighting their way down an aerobridge to get onto a plane when we were all trying to get off it. And if you are one of those fortunate people who actually managed to find the lavatory at Charles de Gaulle, please write and let me know, with maps if possible.

Compared with Paris, London's Heathrow airport has a sort of raffish World War Two charm. It's almost as if Dougie Bader, with his tin legs, had just taken off in his Spitfire to take a crack at the Hun. It was in fact laid down in the 1940s and they're still building it. Heathrow can be summed up in three words—grubby, inefficient, congested. If you go there from Australia you'll arrive at the long haul Terminal Three, which is already stretched to capacity and the British government has only just got around to deciding to build a fourth terminal.

There is an alternative to Heathrow, it's Gatwick, which in my experience is slicker and much more efficient, but the Catch 22 is that it's ten million miles from central London. Makes you think how lucky we are having Mascot only a half hour's drive from the city centre.

But Heathrow is a paragon of efficiency compared with Rome's Leonardo da Vinci, which is like a long corridor leading straight to a madhouse; or what about Kennedy in New York— a refugee camp full of bad tempered people. But of all the horrors of the world I think Belgrade in Yugoslavia really takes the biscuit. How wonderful to sit calf deep in litter drinking warm beer and eating bits of sausage, while being told for the umpteenth time that JAT 606 is delayed.

Airports in some of the world's most exotic locations are sometimes a bit of a let down. In Tahiti, the girls in grass skirts still dance at the airport to pay for their dental bills because our European diet has played hell with their molars; they open their mouths and you see nothing but gaps. In Katmandu there's a large lump in the middle of the runway and the planes roll up and over it. The terminal buildings, by the way, look like the changing rooms for Western suburbs amateur football team.

My favourite airport has got to be Tufi in New Guinea, where your baggage is carried to a waiting outrigger canoe and you're paddled across to your hut.

And that's another thing about airports, they tend to turn people into single human units and all their inhibitions fall away. There is a common bond in suffering and you'll suddenly find that the guy next to you waiting for the delayed service to Denpasar is going to tell you his entire life story. He'll show you pictures of his kids, give you tips on the stock exchange, ask you home for dinner. But somehow you know the friendship isn't going to last. Because invariably, by the time you both reach your destination he'll be cold and distant and probably won't even say goodbye. That's the thing about airports. They change people.

Burning up the miles

SOME people go to the most extraordinary lengths to prepare themselves for a Jumbo ordeal...the horrors of a long-distance flight. Roughly speaking, there are three sorts of travellers:

1 Those who intend to eat everything given to them, drink the plane dry and then become highly objectionable while drunk.
2 Those who 'dormouse' their way through the flight by taking sleeping tablets.
3 Sensible people, who eat and drink little and try to exercise by walking around the plane and promenading at airports.

You would think that regular travellers would fall into the third category. But some of us never learn. Some years ago, the BBC sent a television crew from London to South Africa. At Heathrow, the cameraman, a seasoned traveller, handed out sleeping pills to the crew for the twelve-hour flight. Barely had the plane's wheels retracted than the entire crew were rigid in their seats, nodding and dribbling. Two hours out, while over the Mediterranean, the plane developed engine trouble and returned to Heathrow. There, the hostesses were unable to wake the crew and wheelchairs were called for to get them off the plane. Still sleeping, they were put to bed at an airport hotel to await the next available flight.

At six the next morning the cameraman woke the rest of the crew with an alarm call. 'There you are, what did I tell you,' he said. 'Here we are in Johannesburg and you didn't even feel a thing.' It was only as the dawn came up and the features of London airport became discernible from his bedroom window that he realised he still had a long flight ahead.

Even more bizarre was the woman who doped herself with sleeping pills when leaving Heathrow and fell instantly into a drugged sleep holding a cigarette in her right hand. As her head lolled forward, the cigarette ignited the front of her heavily lacquered hair, and the hostesses were called to extinguish the incandescent traveller.

Merlin the inflammable

I had rehearsed the moment a million times. What would I do in a hotel fire? Which possessions would I grab as the smoke came curling under the door of my bedroom? Would I be trapped on the balcony as the flames rose around my neck?

Well, the smoke was curling under the door, and there were muffled cries in the corridor. This would have been nasty enough had one been sober. But very few white men are sober in Singapore at one o'clock on a Sunday morning. I had been, as they say, 'on the town' with our man in Singapore, the late, and much missed Tony Joyce. We had done Bugis Street until it would Bugis no more, and staggered home after a few gin slings in the Winston Churchill bar at Raffles. My head felt like a delayed action bomb with the time fuse activated. Another few seconds and it would explode. Then the telephone by my bed rang and an Asian voice said, 'Hotel on fire. Gerroit real quick.' Ah yes, I thought, one of the crew has just seen me get home late and is having a little joke. My head hit the pillow again and I fell back into a drunken slumber. Then the hammering on the door began in earnest. In the doorway stood the cameraman, an Irishman. He wore nothing except his Y-fronts and was carrying $20 000 worth of sixteen millimetre movie camera. 'De hotel's on foir,' he said thickly. 'Get out quick.'

In the corridor I could see people running along with wet handkerchieves over their mouths. This had gone past a joke.

We were on the sixteenth floor and it was a long way down. Which of my possessions should I take with me? The room was in a terrible mess. Socks and underpants lay about the room. I could find one sock, but not the other. My trousers could not be found, so I made it to the lift wearing a Hawaiian flower shirt and a pair of underdaks. 'Don't take de lift,' said Irish. 'Dere could be smoke in de elevator shaft.' So we hoofed it downstairs pursued by a boisterous party of English sailors. In the lobby, hundreds of guests were sitting around in their night attire while outside the fire brigade was practising with the turntable ladder. As the dawn came up we saw that indeed it had been a proper fire, but luckily everyone had survived. It was then that we hit upon a wizard wheeze. We were checking out that day to catch the dawn flight to Bangkok. Did the management expect us to pay for the privilege of being burnt to death. We hailed a passing microbus, piled the equipment on board and hi-tailed it to the airport. I never was asked to pay the bill at the Merlin Singapore. But I'm still missing a pair of socks.

My good mate Tony Joyce died tragically in Africa. He, too, had been out on the binge that night. He was very peeved the next day to find that we hadn't tipped him off about the fire story and that the eye-witnesses were on their way to Thailand.

Plastic Nessie

THERE are two monsters in Loch Ness, Scotland. One generates a good deal of money for the tourist industry, although no one is sure it exists. The other is a large piece of submerged tubing manufactured by a University in the English Midlands. It is what scientists call a wave energy experiment and it is designed to produce electrical energy from the action of the waves. Unfortunately, it bears an uncanny resemblance to Nessie, and has been responsible for many 'sightings', usually by people who have been fortunate (or unfortunate) enough to have had a collision with a bottle of Auld Malt.

The workings of the Sea Clam, as the device was called, were something straight out of Heath Robinson. Seen from a distance it looked like a discarded piece of concrete piping half submerged in the water. When I got closer to it in my rowing boat, I discovered that it was a piece of concrete piping half submerged in the water. The boffins associated with the project were young, bearded and enthusiastic. 'Loch Ness is a natural wave tank,' one of them explained. 'The action of the waves on the bladders forces the air through the reciprocating turbines.' Unfortunately, the turbines weren't reciprocating that day. It was something to do with the waves being, as Stanley Holloway would put it, 'fiddling and small'.

To make a television programme about this highly improbable piece of new technology, we had to row out to it. It cost us

£5 to hire the good ship *Angus* for an hour. I rowed out to the Sea Clam in the gathering Hibernian gloom. Even to someone unacquainted with the workings of wave energy, it was obvious that this clam wasn't going anywhere in a hurry, neither was it about to generate one kilowatt of reticulated electrical energy. Even to my untrained eye it appeared that the large rubber bladders were deflated so the waves would have no effect on them. 'Aye,' said the boatman, 'nay guid will come of it. Nessie won't like it. And neither do I.' It was no secret that the locals regarded the whole thing as a bit of a hoot.

As the mist over Loch Ness thickened, we drove back to Inverness and I looked back at the strange yellow pipe with its blue rubber bladders. It would have to be a drunken Scotsman indeed who mistook this absurd multi-coloured pantomime monster for the real thing. I don't know that it ever produced any electricity for the good citizens of Inverness. Somehow I doubt it. But maybe when the Sea Clam has outlived its usefulness in that great natural wave tank, some enterprising local entrepreneur might find a new use for it as a fairground attraction. I doubt whether the Department of Energy will have any further use for it.

Kashmir

Kashmir, 'The Emerald Green Jewel' of northern India, offers almost everything that a tourist desires—colourful people, beautiful gardens and lakes, leisurely *shikara* or boat rides, endless stores to shop in and, above all, luxurious houseboats. Located high in the mountains, the Vale of Kashmir was at one time a favourite resort of the Moghul emperors, and in the 19th century retired British Army and civil service officers sought to settle down in Kashmir's comfortable and congenial surroundings. The then Maharajah was not at all happy with the influx of the British because there was a chance he might lose his power, so he passed an edict prohibiting them from buying or owning immoveable property in Kashmir. But the British outwitted him and introduced the houseboat which, of course, was mobile.

These days, as far as tourism is concerned, Kashmir and houseboats go together. The commercial houseboats are moored around the edges of Lake Dal and Lake Nagin in Kashmir's capital, Srinigar. Although there are numerous hotels, anybody who doesn't stay on a 'deluxe' houseboat must be suffering from insanity. The 'deluxe' grade, as opposed to A, B, C or D grades, is obligatory. Between $40–$60 a double is all you will pay a day and if you are lucky you will have the boat to yourself. The tariff includes three enormous bedrooms with ensuite bathrooms, a mansion-sized lounge room tastefully furnished with

richly coloured carpets, a carved walnut desk, chairs and lounge
suite, a balcony which could seat ten people overlooking the
lake with its flurry of activity, three hearty meals served in a
formal dining room and a friendly, smiling houseboy.

Even getting across to the houseboat is a joy. The local form
of transport is a gondola-like boat called a *shikara* and there's
really only room for the oarsman and two passengers. Once you
board your *shikara* and leave the busy street life of Srinigar
behind, the scenery takes over. The snowcapped mountains in
the distance, the lilies on the lake and the hundreds of houseboats beckon as you wonder which one is going to be your home
for the next few days. Having reclined Cleopatra-style on
cushioned seats and been leisurely rowed for about half an
hour, friend Susan and I arrived at 'Alexandra Palace'. Aziz the
houseboy welcomed us like long lost friends and we knew the
next few days were destined to be sheer bliss. It turned out to
be not quite as peaceful as we had first suspected. Once we
stepped onto the houseboat, and before we'd even put down our
luggage, we had become prime targets for the commercial
shikaras. They come by in a constant parade to sell groceries,
jewels, furs and even film. The most colourful of all was the
flowerboat where the blooms, according to the enthusiastic
salesman, were no less than 'groovy'. His *shikara* was laden with
tulips, crown lillies, irises, daffodils, hyacinths—all groovy of
course—but the ones with the grooviest price were the daffodils
at 3 rupees a bunch. That's a mere 30 cents. Five bunches were
bought to decorate our palacial houseboat.

The vendors in Kashmir are not as pushy as those in Delhi
and Bombay. They expect you to bargain and they have fun, to
boot, in the process. While we were being rowed by our houseboy
on a sightseeing tour of Lake Dal, we were approached by six
commercial *shikaras*, all at once, wanting to sell their wares at a
'very special' price. 'For you memsahib this beautiful garnet
necklace, special price, 60 rupees.' We were not sure at this
stage whether we really wanted a garnet necklace but Aziz had
decided he was our protector and suggested we hold off for a
while, at least until the price had dropped by half. What a
helpful chap.

The temperature would have been pushing 5° centigrade so

we were rugged up rather like two grannies, but the cold didn't deter us from appreciating the view. By this stage we had made our way into the waterways that run off the lake and it was beautiful, with willows crowding the banks, bright yellow mustard flowers growing wild, plain but attractive wooden houseboats where the locals live, bobbing on the water's edge and women pounding their washing on the stone steps. To our surprise, the houses, although made of mud and brick, were two and three storeys high with jutting wooden balconies and turreted rooftops.

Neither did the cold interrupt the magnificent sound of the Muslim *Azan* floating eerily across the water. In the temples, this sacred pledge to Allah is chanted by specially trained voices and can be heard five times a day. What the cold did do though was make our noses run so it was time for some serious purchasing to be done. We didn't have to look very far for the *shikara* selling groceries and chemist items. The vendors had been following close behind for the past hour. With a make-believe blow of the nose, Susan enquired if he had any tissues on board. Receiving a blank stare she said 'Tissues, to blow your nose.' Of course a lot of Kashmiris have never and will never use tissues or handkerchiefs as it is their custom simply to use their fingers and flick the excess away. It is probably far more healthy when you think about it, but we weren't intending to adopt this custom just yet. And besides we were having fun.

Not half as much as they were though. By now all six *shikaras* had rallied around and with the help of Aziz were trying to decide just what product we did require. Much giggling occurred when we were offered a packet of tampons. Goodness knows how our actions had indicated that was what we wanted. After some more shuffling and opening of cardboard boxes we were presented with a roll of toilet paper which, sure, was a lot closer to the mark. Still couldn't quite work out what our noses had to do with it. Not people known to give up easily, we heard in the background, 'Memsahib, this beautiful necklace, very special price. For you only 50 rupees.' 'No, no,' said Aziz. 'You will get better price.'

Garnets aside, where were these wretched tissues? Our noses were getting desperate and we were just about to make do with the toilet paper when our salesman proudly presented a dusty old box of ladies tissues called 'Julies'. The cellophane was torn and tatty but the contents were intact, so Susan handed over the requested 5 rupees and the sale was completed. Our noses rejoiced.

It was not until we were on our way back to Alexandra Palace and laughing about the whole episode that we noticed a sticker on top of another sticker. The top one read 'Price for sale 5 rupees' but the one underneath read 'Recommended maximum price 2 rupees'. Shrewd businessmen these *shikara* vendors.

To complete a near perfect tourist day, both Susan and I bought a string of garnets for 25 rupees a piece. Not a bad price according to our protector Aziz. You can bet your bottom dollar the recommended maximum price was about 10 rupees but for us they were rupees well spent. Think of the memories those garnets will bring back.

Poor Peter

THE trouble with lions is that you can never find one when you want one, even if you are in a safari camp in Zimbabwe, in darkest Africa. Our exact location was Makalolo Camp in Wankie National Park, Matebeleland, not far from Victoria Falls. Roaming around this enormous reserve of 14 000 square kilometres are some of the largest herds of elephant and buffalo on the African continent. Several parks use combi vans with open tops for game-viewing, but in Wankie they use an open landrover which I think is the ideal vehicle for this purpose. It takes eight people who stand holding the crossbars, your eyeline is equivalent to the top of a giraffe's head and there is no glass or metal restricting your view.

The three landrovers at Makololo are owned by Alan Elliott who has been running the 'Touch the Wild' camp for several years. The camp consists of a row of thick canvas tents, flushing toilets, a dining area and half a dozen jacks of all trades.

Alan was poised by the side of the landrover polishing his heavy calibre full game rifle which he carried for protection, emergency purposes and, I suspect, show. The sun was at the perfect angle, the great white hunter was ready to show us his territory and we were all raring to go. The first stop was at a waterhole where we climbed onto the viewing platform. Alan was busting to display his knowledge and it took only seconds for us to realise how much keener is the eye of the professional game warden than that of the newcomer. 'At a lot of these waterholdes, people just come and look at the obvious. Like, there's a giraffe, there's a kudu, there's a hippo, but I know there are a few things you haven't seen yet,' he explained.

Our myopic friend, Peter, had little or no chance of spotting the less than obvious. The rest of us searched frantically with binoculars but had to wait for explicit directions from Alan before we had any idea that four crocodiles were lying with their tails resting on the water's edge. It was even trickier to spot the kudu—deerlike animals with their mouths in the water. They were not only drinking from the waterhole—they were chewing on clods of mud to extract healthy minerals.

For the next four hours we stopped at many more waterholes and our animal-spotting proficiency certainly improved. It was uncanny how our eyes told us that there was something a little bit different in the distance and it was very rewarding being able to locate a tiny gazelle standing petrified in the shadow of a tree hundreds of metres away. Poor Peter!

Although the animals were used to landrovers passing through their domain, they still wouldn't let us get much closer than a few metres. The zebras and wildebeest in the grazing areas were unperturbed until either the car or someone in it made a sudden move or a loud noise. Giraffes appeared to roam either on their own or in twos, while elephants preferred six or eight in their herds. Seeing elephants in the wild gave me an enormous thrill but the question on everyone's lips was, 'Where are the lions?'

Being a professional in every sense of the word, our great white leader had kept the king of the wild for a mighty climax. 'Did anybody else see him in the shadow of the trees?' he asked. 'See the two zebra on the left and the one on the right?—in between them is a large lion.' I was surprised that the zebras didn't appear to be frightened, but Alan knew their idiosyncrasies. 'The zebra have got the lion in sight. They don't know whether or not he is thinking of driving them into an ambush but they won't panic because they are in open country and if he's going to make a move he has to come through open bush to them. So the zebra have the situation under control,' he explained.

At this stage Alan decided that a little more excitement was
necessary and although it was not usually permitted to leave the
road, we were sensible tourists and he was prepared to take the
chance. Approximately 30 metres from the lion which we'd all
sighted by now (except Peter), the engine conked out due to
vaporisation and suddenly there we were in an open car feeling
like ready prey. After a couple of minutes of extreme nervous-
ness, the engine restarted and Alan commented, 'It's not the
first time it has done this near lions.' Peter quickly replied, 'It's
the first time *I've* done it near lions.'

We were now all in the grasp of safari fever and lions had
become the order of the day. We saw three or four prides,
including some cubs, during the next few minutes. Alan's keen
eye, which was working overtime, suddenly spotted movement
in the long grass. We drove in that direction and found four

lions ripping apart an enormous wildebeest that had just been hunted down. The stench was unbearable as they tore its stomach apart—a macabre yet magical sight.

By now it was dusk and there were probably twice as many animals around as there had been at midday. They were off for a drink at the watering holes, feeling less like ready targets with night approaching. Alan's judgement of where various animals could be found was impeccable. At a smaller than usual water-hole on the way back to camp, six gigantic bull elephants (and I mean gigantic) were enjoying some evening refreshments. Again we drove right up to them, perhaps stopping only 10 metres away this time. The sun was setting directly behind them and in all their splendour they slowly swung their trunks and gave us long stares. For me this was the most imposing and awesome sight of all.

This fabulous day had now come to an end and as we drove off into the theatrical African sunset, Peter was heard to mutter *'Simba gone bwana'*. Poor Peter!

Ice cold in Alex (or stone cold dead in de market)

THE problem of what to do with holidaymakers who snuff it is a constant problem for travel agents. Shuffling off this mortal coil is bad enough when you are at home. But when you are 12 000 miles away it can be a problem.

Some travel agents are better organised than others. It is possible even in Sydney to see the metal coffins being loaded onto the cruise ships before they depart for that final journey to Eternity. For many of the blue rinse set, it's a one-way ticket. Either spouse departs these shores with the full knowledge that only one may return. Take for example the elderly man on a world tour organised by a well known Australian magazine. Most European capitals had been visited at breakneck speed. London, Brussels, Amsterdam, Paris and finally Rome. It was in the Eternal City that the old timer had started to feel a bit dicky, but then it was probably the stress of the journey that caused it. Nothing that a lie down, a cup of tea and an aspirin wouldn't cure.

As it happened the tour party had a three-day stopover in Rome. At the end of the first day the old man went to that Vale from which no traveller returns. No one expected to see the wife rejoining the coach when it left two days later. The old lady did not seem a bit perplexed and sat with her hands in her lap contentedly gazing out of the window. 'And, er, where is your husband...' ventured a fellow traveller. 'Did you complete the er, arrangements...?'

'Oh yes,' said the old girl brightly. The fellow traveller persisted. 'And did you have the, er, ceremony in Rome...?' 'Oh yes,' said the lady, 'but Harry's travelling back with us.' She pointed gaily to the luggage rack which contained a funeral urn.

Camel caravan

THE Indian desert state of Rajasthan is well known for its pink city of Jaipur and the Lake Palace Hotel in Udaipur, the location for the James Bond film, *Octopussy*. But its most beautiful and least publicised assets are the desert itself and the villagers who inhabit that vast expanse. For centuries camel caravans have crossed the sand dunes for trading purposes, and these days tourists can follow a similar route.

After a three hour train journey from Delhi, camel safari members reach the camel-breeding town of Bikaner where the camels and their drivers are introduced. This particular group comprised fourteen Australians, fourteen camel drivers, two cooks and fifteen general helpers. On the outskirts of the desert, Bikaner was the perfect spot for testing one's camel-riding ability, and everyone spent a few introductory hours riding round an enormous sandpit. The 'homemade' saddles weren't *quite* soft enough and, no, it wasn't like riding a horse as you had the driver sitting up front controlling the reins and providing something for you to hold. Light cotton garments and 'Milanese' knickers were the fashion of the day. The loose clothing kept you cool and the special pants were designed to minimise any chafing on the behind. I started off at the end of the camel string and it certainly was a fabulous sight to see the long line of camels plodding off into the desert. Two water carts drawn by camels followed behind with a tiny goat attached by a rope bringing up the rear of the caravan.

After four days riding from Bikaner, the desert had changed dramatically. The flat sand and stones had graduated into beautiful rolling dunes and the villages had become smaller and more primitive. Each night we camped just a few metres away from a village and its water supply. Once, when we had set up camp on top of some high sand dunes, the village chief invited us to look over his village. The round huts were made from a combination of mud and cow dung and most had thatched roofs. Even though these tourist caravans travel across the Rajasthan desert a couple of times a year, the route changes and the people in this remote village had never seen Europeans before, let alone people riding camels in this harsh environment just for fun. They must have thought it was absurd!

Naturally they wouldn't let us get too near, or take close-up photographs. One difficult moment occurred when we were offered water from the village well. The air was hot and we were all thirsty but our constitutions simply couldn't cope with the different minerals in the Indian water. Some of us politely refused and others pretended to sip from the side of the drinking vessel so as not to offend these gentle, generous Rajasthanis.

All deserts are said to be magical and mystical and the stars are always bigger and brighter. But the Rajasthan desert has an added appeal—its people. Most deserts are virtually uninhabited but in Rajasthan we would often be riding along with nothing but sand in view when over a dune would appear two or three women clad in vividly coloured saris and with water pots on their heads, heading for a distant well. The women always wear saris of bright yellows, reds, greens and blues in Rajasthan and their arms and necks are invariably choked with the intricate local jewellery. This colour presents an incredible contrast to the neverending monochromatic sand.

On average, we would walk, or sometimes trot, 20 kilometres a day or as far as we could get in eight hours. Our 'specially designed' camel-riding gear was certainly not doing the trick for me. My behind was so sore on the fourth day of our ten-day expedition that I decided to walk for a while. Initially this seemed like a wise decision but it turned out that even to walk was almost impossible as the pain was too great! My driver was the leader of the camel train and was obviously no fool. The saddle was constructed of his bedding including a thin mattress, an even thinner pillow and a couple of worn-out blankets. Quite enough one would have thought to soften the top of this dromedary. And it should have been adequate except *he* had 90 per cent of it! I can't say I blame him as it was his bedding and he *was* the leader, but I did wonder how the honeymoon couple in the group were faring.

All in all, our group was rather enjoying this adventure through the timeless Indian landscape. One woman from Canberra couldn't quite get over the fact that this part of India was so clean and that the village women kept their huts spotless. She expected filth from top to bottom. But the woman from Melbourne who insisted on singing around the campfire *every* night had to be severely dealt with when even the Indians couldn't cope with another rendition of 'Waltzing Matilda'.

The goat, who had soon become everyone's pet, had had his neck rope lengthened so he was pretty happy. The chief cook, a sherpa from the mountains, had found his curried eggs, boiled potatoes and dhal were appreciated by the tourists, so he was happy too. We hadn't eaten any meat so far on the trip which didn't seem to bother anyone and it was only when we sat round the fire savouring the smell of a freshly cooked curry that we realised the smile had been wiped from the face of our pet goat. No one could eat the curry that night even though it smelled absolutely delicious. At later meals the goat curry was devoured. The clean desert air creates a healthy appetite.

It's pretty unusual for most people to rate the end of any trip as the highlight but, in this case, our arrival at our destination, the desert town of Jaiselmer, was majestic. From our campsite on the last night we could see the town sitting on the horizon and for most it was a sad thought knowing that the camels and drivers we had come to know so well would soon be leaving us. Communication had been in sign language and the camels had retained that customary haughty look, but they had just starting responding to our commands of 'zut' (which means 'get up you lazy bugger') and in some cases they seemed to have befriended the Australian riders.

Jaiselmer loomed in the distance. The high and sturdy walls resembled a fort. The town had been built with garrisons and guns to keep out any invaders from the north but somehow it seemed to welcome *us*. The entrance to Jaiselmer is a large, double-gated opening in the sandstone walls, and that is where we began to hear the proverbial honking of horns so common in India. The offending machines were small scooters and trishaws and, after initial alarm from the desert-tamed camels, we slowly made our way up the cobbled street to the town square. There we parted company with our camels and drivers and to say thank you, gave them each some well earned money and a token gift, the most successful being a Swiss army knife.

With feet securely on the ground and goods and chattels slung over our shoulders, we were escorted through the most charming town I have ever seen. Centuries ago, Jaiselmer's strategic position on the camel train routes between India and Central Asia brought great wealth to the town and this opulence is still obvious. There are magnificent mansions all exquisitely carved from a golden yellow sandstone. Known as 'havelis', the most elaborate is the Patwon ki Haveli which stands in the narrowest of lanes. The old town is completely surrounded by a high wall and within this rises a hill on top of which is a hotel called the Jaiseal Castle Hotel, located a few metres past the Jain temples, built in the 12th and 13th centuries. We checked in, and for 30 rupees a night (about $3), we spent the next two days resting our sore bodies. And what a way to end a holiday, sitting like magnificent maharajahs on top of a mighty fort, lazily sipping pink gins as the sun slowly set over the Rajasthan desert.

Great hotels of the world

I shall always remember with affection the Hotel Annapurna in Kathmandu. Nowhere else in the world is there such a concentration of employees all dedicated to the same cause: inefficiency.

Kathmandu itself is a delight. Visitors who live in cities of concrete and glass will find Kathmandu like stepping into a time warp. The narrow streets with their mud and timber houses are straight out of the Middle Ages. There are some great little restaurants selling Russian, Chinese and Indian food. There are pie shops and junk shops and dope shops selling chunks of marijuana big enough to blow your head off.

The Annapurna, however, is designed for European and American clientele who want to insulate themselves from all that squalor. First impressions are good—a uniformed gurkha salutes you as you pass through the front door; the rooms are well appointed with stunning views of the Himalayas. But the most entertaining feature of the Annapurna is its restaurant. Never have I ever seen so many waiters. No less than three separate functionaries ushered me to my table. There was lots of bowing and scraping and 'Good morning, Sair-ing.' It all looked very promising. The maitre d', a haughty Sikh, glided from table to table like a swan. But as the days wore on, it became patently obvious that what passed for organised efficiency was merely a thin veneer concealing confusion and ineptitude on a Titanic scale.

For a start, none of the waiters could understand any English. Conversations went like this:

'Do you understand English?'

'Oh, yes, indeed I do.'

'Very well. I would like scrambled eggs, orange juice, coffee. Got it?'

'Oh yes, indeed.' Our waiter had been scribbling on his pad. But when I looked over his shoulder I saw that he had written nothing. Like many Nepalese he was too polite to offend by saying that he didn't understand. This essay in non-communication went on for several days. If you ordered eggs you got porridge. If you ordered fried eggs, you got cornflakes. Sometimes you got nothing at all, and the waiters lurked behind the pillars, always with those infuriating, obsequious smiles. If you complained, the maitre d' would bawl out a waiter in front of you, or even attack him. Once I saw him push a waiter through the swing doors into the kitchen, while he was carrying a plate of haddock. At first it was hugely amusing. After three days of this, with breakfast taking at least an hour from go to whoa, everyone had had enough.

Next to our table was a party of French tourists, who, like us, were long suffering. A Madame Lelouch rose to her feet, speechless with rage. It is the only time in my life I have ever seen anyone go puce. She grabbed the waiter by the throat and shook him like a rag doll. So tedious did it become waiting for our meals that our group decided to entertain ourselves. In the centre of the dining room was a bandstand with an ancient drum kit, a piano and a three-stringed double bass. When I enquired where the musicians were, the maitre d' explained that they were 'in Darjeeling on their holidays'. Three of us took over the piano, the drums and the bass and were happily plonking away when the maitre d' approached us. Solemnly he announced: 'Will you please stop playing your guitar. There have been complaints.'

Coldly, I returned his gaze. 'This is not a guitar, it is a double bass. Not only that, our music is a good deal better than your service. And I am a house guest.'

The Chunnel

A few years ago, people in England were saying that it would soon be possible to drive to Paris for lunch. What I'm talking about is the Channel Tunnel—the trendies call it the Chunnel—which has been talked about ever since Christ wore rompers and it now looks as if it might really happen.

There's this bit of water, you see, called the English Channel and those 23 miles between Dover and Calais separate the upright, noble and perfectly wonderful English from the nasty, treacherous, garlic-smelling French. The English call it 'abroad' and George V used to say, 'I hate abroad.'

Yes, would you believe it, after 179 years they have finally decided that there is to be a Channel tunnel. But times are hard and there's no way the British government is going to fork out a cent for it. It is up for grabs from private enterprise.

There are four serious options. A single track rail tunnel costing eleven hundred million dollars, a double track rail tunnel costing two thousand, two hundred million, a road bridge costing four thousand million and a road bridge and road tunnel combined costing five thousand six hundred million.

Does this mean that Britain is no longer an island, I hear you cry. Well, I'll believe it when I see it. Let's face it, the track record of British and French collaboration is hardly good. It all started to go bad with William the Conqueror, then there was Agincourt, that nasty business with Joan of Arc, not to mention

Mers El Kebir and the destruction of the French fleet in North Africa during World War Two. And what about the New Hebrides.

But what are the positive returns of a Chunnel? Well, the people backing the rail tunnel project reckon they will get between 11 and 15 per cent return on their money over 50 years. It will be good for tourism too; trade will be speeded up between Britain and Europe and they say it will mean fewer trucks on the road.

Until now of course, the Brits have lived in splendid isolation. This septic isle, this blessed plot, this fortress built by nature etc. But the game's up. What Napoleon and Hitler failed to do will be achieved by the stroke of a bureaucrat's pen, and out of a hole in the ground will pour hundreds of small men with moustaches, all sounding like Moriarty in the Goon show.

But assuming it is a tunnel, what happens in mid-Channel when the French cars change over to the left-hand side of the road and the English change to the right? Just imagine if it happened here. You could whip out the Kingswood on Sunday arvo and nip over to France for a quick glass of Beaujolais and the odd escargot. But somehow, I can't help being a bit sceptical. The British and French have never been known to agree on anything.

Oh yes, I can see the opening ceremony in 1988. Margaret Thatcher and President Mitterrand cracking a bottle of Veuve Cliquot to open the escalator joining the English Channel Tunnel to the French Channel Bridge. *Entente cordiale*, my Aunt.

La Torera

GEORGE Negus and I both have one thing in common. We both like George Negus. In the four years since '60 Minutes' started, George has emerged as certainly the most visible of the reporters; unashamedly Ocker he is a good interviewer, a loyal companion and a terrier after a story. Having said all that, I wouldn't put the command of languages (foreign languages that is) high on his list of priorities.

For reasons which are now obscure, we were in Spain, making a film about Spain's only lady bullfighter, Maribel Atienzar. This raven-haired, black-eyed beauty was the biggest thing in bullfighting since Cordobes. Not only did she have the guts to face the bull but she also looked good. Maribel Atienzar had even coined a new word in Spanish. 'La Torera' (the *female* bullfighter). Five years before, a woman fighting a bull would have been unthinkable in Spain. But Maribel was bombarded with flowers everywhere she went. She commanded a following as big as any pop group.

Maribel and her parents had moved into a smart apartment in Albacete in central Spain. Maribel's mother looked suspiciously at us when she opened the door. The tall one with glasses looked harmless enough. But what about the one with the Zapata moustache and the cowboy boots. Surely he was no suitor? And certainly with boots like that he was not a good Catholic?

'*Ingles?*' she enquired. 'No,' I said. 'Australiano.' Reluctantly, she admitted us to the hall where a large stuffed bull's head stared down from the wall. Later, we were shown into the family room where Maribel was entertaining a group of fans. The Australianos were treated with a good deal of curiosity. Neither George nor I spoke any real Spanish, but she warmed to the Balmain cowboy. So a working relationship was established. The deal was that we should follow her around for a few days and film her fighting at various *corridas*.

Anyone who has been to a bullfight will tell you what an *abbatoir* it is. The marvel was that tiny Maribel had enough strength to plunge a sword into the bull's neck. Maribel looked stunning in her pale blue, skin-tight suit of lights. We were wondering, though, how long it would be before a bull's horn pierced one of those shapely thighs, and with it her femoral artery.

At some part in this heartwarming story of Death in the Afternoon I wanted to show on camera the burgeoning relationship between George and Maribel. The opportunity came when we stopped for lunch one day on the road to Alcazar de San Juan. Maribel had injured her arm and it was in a sling, but had agreed to fight at a small country *finca*. The town was so small there was not even a proper bullring. The farmers had simply formed an arena with their trucks and carts, and Maribel was the star turn.

The luncheon was in an open air restaurant, and Maribel was protected by her brothers. The family sat down to lunch and engaged in a family business discussion from which George was excluded. How then to involve George with Maribel when he didn't speak the lingo? I took him on one side and explained that we needed a bit of 'involvement'. 'OK mate,' said George, 'I know what you want. You want me to chat her up a bit. No worries.'

We started rolling the camera. The beautiful, dark-eyed Maribel was still talking to her brothers and ignoring George. Deliberately, George filled two glasses with sangria, touched the *torera* on the elbow and bawled in her ear, 'Hey Maribel, *PARLAY VOUS FRANCAIS?*'

Maribel shot him a glance. '*Non*,' she said, and carried on with her conversation.

The music man

IRELAND has two great tin whistle players. One of them is Micho Russel. The other one isn't.

Micho Russel lives in one of the most beautiful parts of western Ireland, at Doolan, near the famous Cliffs of Moher. To collectors of true ethnic Irish folk music, his name is legendary. 'You must,' said the man from the Irish Tourist Board, 'go to hear Micho play. The Germans came to record him for an LP. He's famous all over the world.'

The Cliffs of Moher were shrouded in mist, and the road was awash. Ireland is a country of sunshine and showers, but on this day it was raining not only downwards, but from left to right and occasionally upwards as well. The windscreen wipers were working overtime. Micho Russel, it transpired, was not on the phone. But you couldn't possibly miss his house. It was 'tree miles down de road, over de bridge, turn right, turn left, can't miss it. If you lose your way, just ask.' That was all very well, but how does one ask the way if there's no one to ask? Finally I stopped a man driving some cattle. He wore a flat cap and had what can only be described as unruly front teeth, which may have accounted for his speech patterns. He bore a resemblance to John Mills when he played the idiot in *Ryan's Daughter*, but then Ireland seems to be full of people like that.

All we could establish from Cro-Magnon man was that Micho's house was painted white. A short time after that we saw a man lounging in the open door of a white house, staring at the teeming rain. Wading across the quagmire that passed for his front garden, we hailed him. Was he Mr Russel, de flute man? Yes, he assented, he was de same. Could we record on our portable cassette recorder the mystery and wonder of his playing? Yes, we could.

Inside the lowly kitchen, stained undergarments were strung across the fire, steaming. Mr Russel solemnly screwed together his flute and launched into his first song. 'De name of de tune,' he said, earnestly, 'is "De silver Spear"'. It was dreadful. Although we enthusiastically tapped our feet, it was obvious that Mr Russel was no James Galway. Perhaps he would like to try the tin whistle?

Rummaging among the sardine tins, used biros and old fag packets on the shelf, Mr Russel unearthed his tin whistle and then committed brutal murder on a tune called 'The Wind That Blows the Barley'. It was the worst bit of tin whistle

playing I had ever heard. Even Blind Freddie could tell that Mr Russel wouldn't be doing a gig at the Carnegie Hall. The church hall perhaps.

I gave him five Irish pounds. He wasn't worth it, but I didn't have any small change. As we paused in the doorway, I ventured a last question. He was *the* Mr Micho Russel, the famous internationally known recording artist?

'No,' said Mr Russel, 'dat's me brudder. Micho lives down de road, three miles, turn left, turn right, over de bridge, in de white house...'

Midday excess

Drinking at lunchtime in a hot climate has always been my downfall. The Greek captain of the luxury cruise liner had a brother in Melbourne who drove cabs. He had, it appeared, an unlimited stock of Fosters lager in cans, and wished to entertain us on the bridge of the *Stella Solaris*.

We were filming a Greek cruise. It had not as yet been a difficult assignment to produce a ten-minute travelogue while drifting aimlessly from Piraeus via Santorini, Delos to Ephessus, and finally a landfall in Istanbul. As a public relations exercise for the shipping company, the cruise of the *Stella Solaris* had no peer. The five denim clad reprobates who passed for the film crew were spared no luxury. A helicopter had been placed at our disposal. In between shooting languid sequences of the sun sinking below the Bosporus we were offered the finest caviar on the thinnest slivers of toast. The main decision of the day usually had to be made at dinner, whether or not to try the Pouilly Foussé or the Mouton Rothschild.

The captain turned out to be in the words of the camera assistant, a 'ripper bloke'. As we stood on the bridge of the ship, gazing at the traffic passing over the Galata Bridge and downing our eighth beer that lunchtime, it occurred to me that perhaps we should do some work.

Filming in many European countries can be a painful experience. Confronted with many thousands of dollars' worth of camera equipment, the reaction of most customs officials is to confiscate it and then charge an extortionate rate for giving it back. On this trip we had already had film stock impounded in Athens by the customs department, despite the fact that we had a permit to make a film in that country.

We had no such permit to film in Turkey. We decided that we would leave the ship and go ashore to film some general sequences of Istanbul. We mingled among a group of harmless tourists and slipped through the customs post. We passed the customs officers with no problem. It was only when we came under the scrutiny of the unshaven security guard carrying an ancient Lee Enfield 303 rifle that things started to become a little emotional. A tug of war developed over the camera. There appeared to be some *contretemps* as to whether or not it was dutiable. Emboldened by the Fosters, and mindful of the confiscation of our film in Greece, we were slightly bolshy.

The scruffy guard did not understand my execrable French. The sound recordist tried him in German, which he understood.

'Tell him,' I said, 'that we are on a top level mission from the Australian government and if he does not let us through his job is on the line.'

At this point, one member of our party indicated that he needed to relieve himself. Accompanied by the armed guard he was led through the office to the toilet at the rear of the building. To do this he had to pass through an office full of Turkish customs clerks scratching away with quill pens in their ledgers. Thanks to the excessive consumption of beer, our crew member was by now bursting, but the lavatory was already occupied.

Next to the toilet was a small storeroom partitioned off with a bead curtain. Pulling back the bead curtain he surveyed the heap of old customs files. In the centre of the room was a small stepladder and on top of it a large, ornate, Turkish teapot. There seemed to be no other course. Removing the lid our hero filled up the teapot with a pint of the best, then took off into the streets of Istanbul with the guard in hot pursuit.

I can't imagine what the tea tasted like after that, but the whole episode was scarcely likely to improve Turkish-Australian relations.

Black Mak

Outside Limassol in Cyprus there used to be a restaurant called Nazims where you could eat your fill of Middle Eastern delicacies like ladies fingers and hommos. I went there in 1967 with the crew of an RAF transport plane and we drank a considerable amount of rough red wine. Two weeks later, somebody threw a bomb into Nazims and burned it to the ground. Cyprus has always been like that.

On the surface it is an attractive Mediterranean holiday island. But there is always an undercurrent of tension. In its long history Cyprus has been invaded by just about everyone: the Romans, the Greeks, the Turks, the British. And since the sixties it has been a divided nation with Turkish and Greek enclaves and the United Nations keeping them apart.

On 'Travellers Tales' we were pleased to interview the writer Ron Saw, himself a great lover of Aphrodites' Isle. Ron was on holiday in Cyprus when the Turkish fleet invaded. He was sitting eating his breakfast at a hotel in Kyrenia when the Turkish fleet appeared on the horizon and shells started falling on the hotel. Ron spent a horrid few days before he was rescued by the Royal Navy and taken home in HMS *Ark Royal*.

For some years now the British have maintained a big airbase at Akrotiri. The huge runway juts out into the bay and Vulcan V-bombers thunder down to take part in training exercises up and down the Mediterranean. Ever present in the bay were always the Russian trawlers. I don't know what they were trawling for but one of them got stuck on a sandback while I was there and as the tide went out you could quite clearly see that it was bristling with antenna beneath the waterline.

The word in those days was that the Royal Air Force had the atom bomb in Cyprus. It was rumoured that the RAF was going on training flights right up to the border between Turkey and the Soviet Union and that in the event of global nuclear war it would attack Soviet satellite countries leaving the Americans to take out the major targets inside Russia. How true this was I don't know, but while we were on the island there was a fairly nasty incident involving a bomb which fell off a fighter plane and landed in somebody's back garden. Only a few months before in Spain there had been the so-called Palomares incident, when a B-52 had accidentally released one of its H-bombs and covered a wide area with radioactive material.

All this seemed like a good reason to ask the Cypriot leader, Archbishop Makarios, what he thought about his country being used as a nuclear springboard, if indeed it was. Two phone calls later found us at the former Governor's residence in Nicosia waiting to record an interview with his Beatitude. I recall that I had to submit my questions to the Palace in advance because he did not understand English too well. My information was that Black Mak understood as much English as he wanted to, and when the questions started to become curly, then was the time to act dumb.

The British, of course, never cared much for Makarios and once had had him banished in exile to the Seychelles because of his links with the Eoka terrorist organisation. Some believed that this sinister man had the blood of many innocent National Servicemen on his hands.

We cooled our heels in the ante-chamber. Suddenly the door swung open and a small man in a white tuxedo announced: 'Gentlemen, his Excellency the Archbishop'. We set the cane chairs on the lawn and recorded the interview. Makarios, heavily bearded, spoke softly in a sibilant Greek—accented voice. Always there was a faint smile playing around his lips. What did he think of Cyprus being used as a nuclear springboard? He wasn't aware of it, but if there was the bomb in Cyprus, he didn't approve. And what were his feelings about the activities of the underground terrorist organisation known as the National Front? 'They are a dissident minority,' lisped Makarios. 'We have the situation under control.'

That same dissident minority had that week raided a police station in the Turkish sector and stolen some weapons. One had the impression that many people would have liked Makarios's head on a plate. A few weeks after we interviewed him someone shot down his helicopter in the centre of Nicosia. It crashed in the middle of an ornamental fountain. The pilot was shot through the stomach but miraculously Makarios survived. Makarios died a few years ago and is buried in the solid rock at a monastery in the mountains.

Despite the tension, I could very easily go back to Cyprus, with its orange groves and ruins. Cypriots in Australia have told me of the heartbreak they experience by not being able to return to their villages because they are now in the Turkish sector. Some day perhaps Greeks and Turks will live in harmony there. I hope so.

Caledonia, stern and wild

I would like to draw your attention to that sturdy country north of Hadrian's Wall, full of purple mountains and sandy—haired men. I'm referring, of course, to Scotland, Caledonia—stern and wild, the land of shortbread, tartan and tweed and bad jokes about the indifferent quality of Scottish poetry or third-degree burns. The Scots are convinced that their country has been exploited and betrayed and these are attitudes they will express to any foreigner. Don't get me wrong, Scotland has some terrific attractions for the Aussie tripper. It just seems to me that the Scots are not all that keen to share them with anyone.

This quality is what the Scots call dour, a fundamental mistrust of outsiders. Mind you, it helps if you know the ropes. John Cleese of 'Fawlty Towers' fame tells the story of when he visited the Vice Chancellor at St Andrews University, the oldest university in the world. He was asked if he wanted to share a wee dram of a 300—year old malt, and made the fundamental mistake of asking for water in it. 'Mister Cleese,' said the Vice Chancellor, 'a great many clever men have gone to a great deal of trouble to get the water oot of that Scotch.' Need I say more.

On the subject of whisky, of which there are several hundred different brands compared with what is available in Australia, the Scots seem to apply a double standard: they either love it with a besotted passion or detest it as an instrument of the devil, or both. Mind you, they know how to enjoy themselves. Just look at Robbie Burns, permanently drunk, always running after girls and dead at thirty-five. These days he would probably have been a television personality with shoulder length hair.

The Scots are themselves great travellers and business men. When you look at the large corporations of the world in America, Britain or New Zealand, they are controlled by Scots or Jews. There has always been poverty in Scotland and its slender population has been further denuded by large scale immigration to other lands.

The rigours of the Scottish climate, however, are much exaggerated. Scotland gets the Gulf Stream from South America and England doesn't. But just look at what else Scotland has given the world: penicillin (Fleming), metal bridges (Telford), philosophy (David Hume), the steam engine (James Watt) television (John Logie Baird). The list is endless, and Scottish culture has spread all over the world.

If it is fine hotels you want then Scotland has some splendid examples. In Inverness there is the Station Hotel which was restored by British Rail and boasts a splendid staircase and a fine restaurant with a wine cellar than even stocks Australian wines. And it was in Inverness that I saw the cutest name for a coffee house. It was called the Ness-Café!

Konitcheewa

Tony Baldwin, apart from being an ABC announcer, presenter of 'Slightly Out to Lunch', fluent in Japanese and French and also an accomplished jazz pianist in the style of Art Tatum, is also a collector of rare 78 rpm jazz records. His quest for the black shellac led him to the Japanese city of Osaka, where he had heard there was a large warehouse full of rare material, all going for a song.

Compared to Tokyo, which is all concrete and glass, Osaka is more provincial, and the pace of life is slower. Europeans are perhaps not quite so visible as in other cities. Thus it was, as Tony browsed among the 78s that he felt a light tap on his shoulder. The proprietor was indeed honoured that he had visited his store. He was sorry he had found nothing to his liking. But perhaps as he had come so many miles, could they not dine together?

Tony accepted the dinner invitation, which consisted of many sakis and even more glasses of Japanese vodka. He and his host got steadily drunker without eating anything. It was only when they were both nearly horizontal that mine host announced, '*Now* we go to dinner.'

Dinner was at home, with wifey. It is unlikely that Japanese wives carry rolling pins, but if she had owned one, Mrs Tanaka would surely have used it. Instead she took one look at the reeling duo and banished them to the municipal bath-house to sober up.

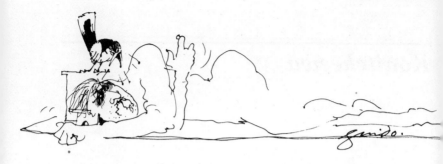

'I had been to Japan before, so I realised that one did not have to take a cake of soap,' Tony told me. Some hours later, having been pampered by geishas, and all their parts washed, they returned to Mr Tanaka's home to be fed and put to bed. Tony was put to bed in Mr Tanaka's room, and Mr Tanaka slept on the couch. Mr Tanaka was no doubt happy to have given up his bed. There is no greater honour in Japan than showing hospitality to a stranger; and no better excuse for coming home drunk and incapable.

Pleasant as it is to be wined and dined Japanese style, there is no greater hangover than that caused by warm saki. But Mrs Tanaka had planned her own revenge. As Tony held his throbbing head the next morning, a pet Mynah bird stood on the bedside table, bellowing into his ear. Kon-itch-ee-wa? Konitcheewa?

Noblesse obliged

WHEN I was a young reporter in England, I had the great misfortune to inherit the society column on a fairly obscure provincial Sunday paper. For a month or so I became 'Alertus'.

The duty of Alertus was to report on the behaviour of the Upper Classes, the Landed Gentry and what Evelyn Waugh called The Bright Young Things. The trouble was that by the time I got the job, most of Britain's peers were penniless and the Bright Young Things now lived in council houses. It was the story of my life. Saddled with an appalling provincial accent, I had spent years trying to sound like David Niven when suddenly it became fashionable to sound like Ringo Starr.

'No matter,' said Fred the Editor, 'that you are working class. I want you to report upon the goings on of the nobs. I want to know how the other half lives. Get plenty of debs and lords in it, doing stupid things. Ring up a few archdeacons. They're always good for a laugh.'

In desperation, I rang every peer in *Debrett's Peerage*. Most of them put the phone down when they heard my urban inflections. The only one who would speak to me was the Marquis of Hall, Warwickshire and possibly the model for Monty Python's original Upper Class Twit. 'How frightfully nice of you to call,' he gushed down the blower. Christ, I thought, I'm in.
you to call,' he gushed down the blower. Christ, I thought, I'm in.

The Marquis was always good for a tale. He was always doing the silly things that marquises do, like employing some dopey hippy to paint the staircase in psychedelic colours (whatever happened to psychedelia?), or giving his son, the Earl of Yarmouth a batman cape for Christmas (whatever became of Batman capes?)

Years passed and I came to Australia. Flicking idly through a British Tourist Authority brochure I discovered that Hugh Edward Conway had fallen upon hard times and was down to his last million. That noble pile, Wagley Hall (the Marquis could never sound his Rs), was in hock for heaps. So the old boy had decided to rent out the place, charging Americans 50 quid a time for bed and breakfast.

Curiously, when I rang him up from Sydney, he actually claimed to remember me. 'How nice of you. After all this time. Come now, the flowers are in bloom.'

We went. Hugh Edward Conway greeted us in the not-so-Great hall waring faded blue jeans and a darned tee shirt. Smirking, he led us on a tour of the house pointing out the Woobens in the Wed Dwawing Woom, the Jade Duck stolen during the Boxer Uprising in Peking and the 40 foot long drapes in the Gween Dwawing Woom. Everything looked a bit tatty, in fact some of the rooms had nothing in them at all. 'Look at those windows,' he said. 'I mean, one simply can't put up pieces of net. Those curtains are velvet and they alone cost me £500.'

I made sympathetic noises. The cameraman muttered something about half the people in England not even having jobs, let alone velvet curtains. 'Oh, it's a Socialist, is it?' shrieked his Lordship. 'How touching. You think we do nothing I suppose. You think I'm a bit of vestigia from another age, is that it?'

It was then that the Marquis put out his hand and demanded 50 quid for showing us around the hall. 'Thanks very much for the interview,' he said, 'but my time is very precious.'

I never did get invited to stay the night with Hugh Edward Conway in the West Wing or possibly the Wed Dwawing Woom. Still, come the Revolution you never know.

'Diamonds are some girls' best friend'

THERE are some places in the world where it helps to be rich, or at least to have the sort of credit limit on your plastic card that means you don't have to leave town when you get the bill. St Thomas, in the US Virgin Island group, is such a place. One of the large neon signs in the main street reads 'The Largest Jewellery Store in the World'. Diagonally opposite, another sign screeches 'The Biggest and Best Perfumery in the Entire Universe'. Whether or not this is true is irrelevant because when you look through the front doors you are unable to focus on the rear of the stores. They are absolutely gigantic.

I have never been all that keen on owning expensive jewellery. I've always considered it a very pretentious way of proving incredible wealth. But I am never too proud to investigate prices, so I entered the largest jewellery shop in the world and walked towards the pearl section. I desperately wanted to head for the diamonds but I knew I'd be spotted as a phoney—the numbers on my credit card haven't yet been worn down by constant use.

Fully expecting a brassy American accent, I was pleasantly surprised when a Cockney voice asked, 'Are you interested in a string of real pearls or something more basic?' I replied, 'Yes, how much is that single strand there in the corner?' She replied, 'Three thousand US dollars madam.' 'They're absolutely adorable, aren't they?' I mumbled, as I shuffled off.

Then, on my right, I overheard a tall, goodlooking American woman say, 'They sure are pretty, aren't they Chaz?' Her equally goodlooking husband instantly replied 'Sure, you waaan'em honey?' She was pointing at three strands of enormous pearls that were so long one would have tripped over them if they'd been round one's neck. Perhaps they would have suited her but they weren't quite what I was after.

Tourists were brandishing credit cards left, right and centre. Americans use the shopping facilities in St Thomas as the French might in London when the sales are in full flight. Still, you don't have to buy pearls, diamonds, watches or gold to strike a bargain on this island. Top brand perfumes and makeup products are available for half the price you'd pay in Australia. Just ask American Express. My statement can prove it and I didn't have to leave town when I received the bill. What a pity!

Fishermen beware!

CINEMATOGRAPHER Mike Dillon has an impressive list of film achievements as long as his arm. It includes *Journey into the Himalayas, Birdmen of Kilimanjaro* and *From the Ocean to the Sky*, the last of which covered the journey with Sir Edmund Hilary and sixteen crew and helpers along the entire length of the Ganges River in India. They did this 2500-kilometre trip, from the river mouth to the actual source, high in the Himalayas, in jet boats—a refined type of speedboat which skims across the water. The lifetime ambition of most Indians is to travel the length of the Ganges and because Hilary is well known in India, tremendous crowds of people gathered at the water's edge to catch a glimpse of the people embarking on this ultimate pilgrimage.

For Mike, the biggest surprise of the trip was in the mangrove swamps at the delta, where they came across an unusual tiger. Last century there were around 100 000 tigers in India but the maharajahs and others turned most of them into rugs and wall hangings. Now there are only 2000 left and approximately 200 of them have migrated to these swamps. Mike explained, 'They've learnt how to drink brackish water and they've adapted their diets to eating crabs, fish and, indeed, fishermen. Twenty pounds of food a day just about keeps them happy, and with nothing much else around, they tend to eat fishermen. We were told they devour about 50 a year!'

This obviously meant caution at all times, so the forestry department provided the protection of a launch as sleeping quarters. After five days no one had sighted even one tiger and they had given up the idea of ever doing so. In fact they were starting to question whether tigers even existed when, on the sixth day, someone noticed what looked like a bit of driftwood floating in the middle of the river. 'On closer inspection it was black with yellow stripes,' explained Mike. 'We tried to get as close as was safe to film while it was swimming across the 400-metre wide river. Another thing they've adapted to is swimming and they can apparently swim up to a kilometre.'

This rather obliging tiger swam to the bank followed by Mike in the jet boat and as he recalled, 'I knew that these tigers could leap 6 metres so I stayed exactly 6.1 metres away and captured wonderful shots of this rarely-seen tiger. Most of the forestry people who'd been there for years had never seen one.' So Mike Dillon scooped the pool. And just imagine a tiger that eats fish and fishermen and then goes for a refreshing swim.

Traditional England

I was intrigued by a recent story of the gang of punk rockers in London who stuck one of their mates to Vauxhall Bridge with Superglue. Those of course, who have written this off as a piece of larrikinism couldn't be further from the truth. Sticking your mate to a bridge is just one of the bizarre and ancient customs which can be observed by the tourist in England. In fact the old country is a veritable treasure trove of traditions... some of them dating back as far as 1973. In addition to sticking your mate to a bridge, there's nailing Grandma to the microwave oven, pop rivetting uncle to the Hills hoist or welding Aunty to a number 16 bus.

But seriously folks, in the UK there's a loony custom for just about every square mile. As a cub reporter, I remember being sent out to cover a pack of jokers called the Abbott's Bromely Horn Dancers. They are a group of fellows who, on a certain day of the year, strap antlers to their heads and jump around the village green shouting in a language that no one can understand. It is one of those traditions passed on from father to son and no one can remember why. The year I went, there was bad blood between the old man and the son and they were muttering about giving it up.

Apart from all the obvious celebrations, like Guy Fawkes night and maypole dancing, there are some that would only appeal to a dedicated nutter. At a place called Hungerford in

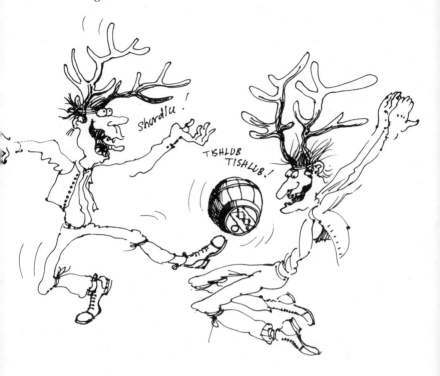

Berkshire they stick an orange on top of a pole, encircle it with spring flowers and go around the town selling oranges for a penny each and asking all the girls for a kiss. These are the so-called Hocktide Tutti Men. The object of the exercise is to get enough pennies to buy grog, although now that two beers cost you over a pound, it can't exactly be a fun happening.

At a place called Hallaton in Leicestershire they go in for bottle kicking and hare pie scrambling. The bottles are not bottles, they are small barrels of beer. There are two teams, any number of players and the object is to kick the barrels over a river into your territory.

A lot of these customs in fact, seem to be a simple excuse to get a bit Brahms and Liszt. At Ashburton in Devon they have a day of the year when they appoint all the ale tasters, bread weighers, pig drivers and scavengers of markets. And what fun the ale tasters have. All they have to do is visit every pub in town and sample the ale.

I could go on. I probably will. On Shrove Tuesdays at a place called Olney in Buckinghamshire they have a pancake race. All the ladies run through the town tossing pancakes in their frying pans and the winner gets a kiss from the vicar and a prayer book. Then there is the Eton wall game at Eton School, which even the players don't understand. Turning the Devil's Boulder at Shebbear in north Devon, not to mention Up Helly Ah in the Outer Hebrides, where they burn a Viking longboat. So the punks with the Superglue are obviously maintaining the great British tradition.

What about the scenery?

CARIBBEAN islands may be a dime a dozen if you live in the United States of America, but for Australians planning a holiday, they are a matter of real money. Throw a few thousand dollars together and you too can experience the glamour, the excitement—even the poverty—of the wonderfully exotic islands of the West Indies. One of the places I visited was Antigua, the birth place of the great cricketer, Vivian Richards, and we arrived just three days after his victorious return from Down Under.

As tourists, the first thing we did was to jump into a tour bus and ask our friendly driver to take us around the island and show us the significant sights. To me, a diehard Aussie, it was more than acceptable for the first point of call to be the street where Vivian Richards was born. Another street, closer to the centre of town and where his father and mother now live, is called Vivian Richards Street.

Our driver was ecstatic at having scored Australian tourists, with more than a vague idea of cricket, who were prepared to let him froth at the mouth about Antigua's super hero. 'Welcome home Vivvy' signs were plastered everywhere. Our driver bragged, 'Vivvy can do no wrong...Since he was a young boy he was destined to be a super hero...Antigua is a beautiful, gorgeous, peaceful Caribbean island...Anything you'd like to know about the place?...Don't be shy...Ask any

91

questions and I'll answer them...But sure, Vivvy is a super-star. His father looks just like him. He lives in Vivian Richards Street and he looks just like him.'

We drove down the famous street and stopped in front of Vivian's parent's house. They were probably hiding behind closed doors for fear of being mobbed. We then continued and passed a group of young boys playing raggle-taggle cricket with what looked like a ball made from a coconut, and finally on to the ground where Baptiste was practising to improve on being twelfth man.

Antigua probably has the best beaches in the Caribbean but we weren't about to see them on this particular tour. Cricket was in the air and nothing was going to change that. A 'Welcome home Vivvy' sign was strategically placed even at the end of the tour.

The other tourist in the bus was an American man and although he'd suffered in silence he finally mumbled through gritted teeth, 'Isn't there a "super hero" gridiron player to be found anywhere on this goddammed island?'

Frank's big one

I can't pretend that the *Readers' Digest* is one of my favourite publications, but Frank Piasecki is certainly one of my most unforgettable characters.

Frank Piasecki is probably the least well known of the pioneers of the helicopter (the others being Bell and Igor Sikorsky). Nevertheless, Piasecki is highly regarded in the aviation world for his unorthodox designs. It was Frank who designed the 'Flying Banana' helicopter, used in the Korean War. Later, he designed and produced a circular 'Flying Jeep' for the US Army. And, when many others had lost faith in airships, Frank persevered.

It was his idea to attach an airship to four helicopters. The envelope of the airship was to be filled with non–flammable helium, rather than hydrogen, the idea being that the lifting power of the helium would cancel out the weight of the helicopters and enable the so-called *Helistat* to lift very heavy cargoes vertically, like a crane.

Like many of Frank's ideas, it sounded a bit far-fetched, but the US Forestry Commission wanted a new type of aircraft to lift logs, and so they advanced some money to Frank to get his idea going. Frank's *Helistat* took shape in, of all places, Lakehurst, New Jersey, where the ill-fated *Hindenburg* had crashed and burned before the war. I had always wanted to go to Lakehurst. That part of New Jersey is not one of the most exciting parts of the United States, but the prospect of standing on the very spot where the *Hindenburg* burned filled me with excitement.

And what of the man, the cigar-chomping eccentric aircraft designer? We had heard that he was not exactly enamoured of the media. I wrote him letters from Australia; he never replied to them. I sent telexes; these too were never answered. I called him; he refused to take the call. But then journalists don't usually give up that easily.

I stood on the windswept airfield at Lakehurst looking up in wonder at the enormous hangar, built for the *Hindenburg*. We had come 12 000 miles to see Mr Piasecki and his wonderful airship. Surely he wouldn't refuse to see us now? In the gloom of the hangar, which was bigger than Westminster Abbey, we could dimly see the enormous bulk of the uninflated gasbag and the skeletal structure holding the four helicopters to it. Even if we had half the Kleig lights at Universal Studios, there is no way we could have illuminated the Helistat enough to film it. Still we had to try.

We took the movie camera out of its aluminium box and set it up on the tripod. Just at that moment, Mr Piasecki arrived. He looked like a Boxer dog. In the corner of his mouth was a cigar butt. He would have passed for a character out of Damon Runyon any time. I explained that we had come from Australia to film the Helistat. 'I don't care where you've come from,' he snarled, 'get the f...out of my hangar.'

It wasn't his hangar, it belonged to the US Navy, but I wasn't about to argue. I often wonder whether Frank Piasecki has the small fluffy koala I sent him to remind him of the incident. At the time of writing, *Frank's Folly* still hadn't flown, but I live in hope.

The shakiest isles

BEFORE the days of Jumbo jets and Apex fares, Iceland was the sort of place you found yourself dumped in if you were flying across the Atlantic. It was, in fact, the cheapest way to get to the United States from Britain; it cost about 70 quid and you got an optional stopover in Reykjavik, where they put you up in a hotel and even gave you a little sightseeing tour. These days it's rather more accessible than it used to be. You can fly there direct from Florida with Air Bahamas which, for some dubious reason, is Icelandic owned, or you can go from any number of airports in Europe.

When they do the weather forecasts on the BBC there always seems to be a deep depression over Iceland, which probably puts off a lot of people. In fact, the weather's not bad. The summers are cool and the winters are fairly mild because, like Scotland, Iceland is kept warm by the Gulf stream. Every time I have been there it's been raining...they get as much as 30 inches a year in Reykjavik, so much rain in fact that the farmers raise two or three crops of hay every summer.

They call New Zealand the 'shaky isles' but Iceland is even shakier; most of the houses are built of reinforced concrete because of the constant earthquake tremors, and it's got more geysers and hot springs than any other country in the world. That word *guyser*, incidentally, is Icelandic—named after Iceland's most famous hot spring which shoots water 200 feet in the air. According to the ABC pronunciation committee a guyser is a hot spring and a geyser is a tank in the bathroom, or possibly a boring old Icelandic fisherman.

Iceland is the land of the midnight sun—22 hours of sunlight in the height of summer...mid-June. Just think what fun you could have with 22 hours of continuous sunshine...the party would never be over. And what fun they have at Icelandic parties. After you've wolfed down the delicacies, like boiled sheep's head and blood sausages, you can drink the local brew called *skyr*, which is made from milk curds, but could have been distilled from fermented hats. Well, what else is there to do when it rains all the time?

Another curious thing about Iceland is that almost everybody has the same name. You know, it's like Wales, where there are 50 000 Jones's and the only way to differentiate is by adding their jobs to their names. In Iceland, instead of Jones the Bread and Jones the Milk, you get Jonsson the fisherman—to differentiate between the other 50 000 Jonssons.

The whole country, of course, revolves around the codfish. The Icelanders are crazy about cod, salted or unsalted, and they even fight wars over it. It all started when British trawlers started fishing in what the Icelanders claimed was their patch. The only way they can survive economically is by selling fish. Unlike the Lucky Country, they don't have much in the way of natural resources, so it's a case of export or die. Yes, Icelandic cod-pieces are world famous.

I don't think Iceland is about to become the Surfers Paradise of the northern hemisphere. It is a special kind of tourist who would want to go trekking through the glaciers in the pouring rain. But it is a very beautiful place. Or it would be if it would ever stop raining...

Bangkok and all that

BANGKOK is the world's leading centre for what Norman Gunston called 'funny business', and this is probably a good moment to send Grandma out of the room.

Yes, the massage parlour business in Bangkok puts Kings Cross and St Kilda in the shade; there are hundreds of places ranging from the opulent to the degenerate, and if you want to know what business is like you only have to see the middle-aged German businessmen being helped back onto their Jumbo jets at Bangkok airport.

It is no secret that an almond-eyed Thai girl can be rented by the hour, week or even year, and experts in this matter say that they are more feminine and less materialistic than other Asians. In fact, the massage parlours in Bangkok are astonishingly well organised. Some of them even have one way mirrors so that you can make your selection, and all the ladies wear a house uniform and carry a number. It's all a bit cold-blooded, terribly un-sexy and rather sad. Everybody is in on the game in Bangkok, from taxi drivers to bellhops they're all part-time pimps. 'Waiter! Bring me another warm woman—this one's going cold.'

But if you get bored with all that rudeness, you might consider a quick squizz at the wats, bots and prangs. Funny isn't it, even the architecture sounds a bit risqué. No, the wats of course are the little chapels and monasteries. Inside the wats are the bots, the main chapel enclosing the buddhas, and the prangs are the stone pinnacles that look like something out of Disneyland. The Thais take their religion very seriously. They don't place a buddha in anything but the highest place; don't point their feet at one and never, never, climb up one to get a better picture. It's a good way of testing the accoustics in a Bangkok prison.

The Thais also revere their king, the saxophone-playing King Bhumipon; they even sent a man to prison because he called his dog Bhumipon. When he was US President, Lyndon Johnson sat opposite the King with his big Texan tootsies pointing directly at his Majesty. When it was pointed out how rude he was being, LBJ replied, 'That's a lot of baloney.'

Thai food—well there is an immense variety of things to eat, everything from elephant's trunk to monkeys' brains. Hotels too are immensely varied and range from super luxury to those that have hot and cold running cockroaches.

As for learning the lingo, a surprising number of Thais speak English, and in Thai there's even an equivalent to our very own 'she'll be right'—it's 'my pen ry'. Add that to our all-purpose Asian phrase, 'Harro Rigger' and you can't go far wrong. 'Harro Rigger' is of course Thai for 'Hello Digger'.

And to close with a sign seen on the back of a hotel bedroom in Pattaya Beach. 'The Management does not mind you bringing ladies to your room but in the interests of your own safety you should not invite the transvestites.'

My pen ry, mate.

Wales, Wales, bloody great fishes are whales

How about a holiday in Wales, the only place in the world where you don't have to keep up with the Jones's. The only problem is getting away from them. Not just the Jones's but the Davies's, Thomas's, Lloyds's and Williams's. Before we go any further, a word for the serious drinker. The pubs in six areas of Wales are closed on Sundays.

Before you go to Wales you should do your homework. Things have been going downhill for Wales ever since 1536. That was when Henry VIII forbade the use of the Welsh language and made it impossible for people who spoke Welsh to hold high office. The Welsh of course were very clever about this; most of their real names were long and convoluted, with the word 'AP' in the middle of them, which means 'son of'. To confuse the Poms they all adopted the same names, Jones, which after Smith is the second most common name in the world. Today the only way you have of distinguishing one Jones from another is by their jobs. Jones the Death—that's the undertaker, Evans the Bank, Williams the Petrol. You got it? The most bizarre Welsh name I ever heard was the local philosopher. They called him Rees the Elevated Thought.

Any tourist in Wales will know that Welsh as a lanugage is very much alive and well. Unlike Gaelic in Scotland and Erse in Ireland, Welsh is not a dead or even a dying language. Australians cannot speak Welsh, however; their tongues are too short. Let's just start with place names beginning with 'LL', of which there are many. Say for example you want to say Llandudno, or as they pronounce it Llandidno. To say the 'LL' you place the tip of your tongue behind your top front teeth and say 'THL'. See what I mean?

Wales is a smashing place so long as you're fond of singing, which the Welsh do far too often, far too loud and flat. Everyone in Wales is a frustrated tenor or baritone, and next to fighting, religion and rugby, singing is the most popular pastime.

Wales is a great country for backpacking, pony trekking or climbing, but a bit light on dining out and good wines. However, the fish is good—especially the local salmon and trout, and they make a type of bread from seaweed called laver bread which is quite acceptable, if you like that sort of thing.

Wales is indescribably pretty. Three of the ten national parks in the UK are in Wales—Snowdonia, the Pembrokeshire coast and the Brecon Beacons. The castles are great too, built either to keep the English out or the Welsh in, depending on your point of view.

Go to Larne where Dylan Thomas is buried. Larne is supposed to be the village on which Thomas based *Under Milkwood*. Great little place. Or Tenby and Saundersfoot in Pembrokeshire. Best little suntrap in the British Isles. And the pubs closing on Sundays isn't too much of a problem. Residents in hotels can still have a drink and so can their guests.

But please make an effort to learn a bit of the language, even if you cover your friends with saliva as Prince Charles did.

The seven wonders of the world

I don't know if you have noticed lately but a lot of the world's major tourists attractions are in really bad shape. The other day I was pointing the Polaroid at the Parthenon and I noticed how tacky it was looking.

No, it's not just Ayers Rock that is wearing away with all those feet going up it. The National Trust in England has shown grave concern over the numbers of tourists going round its' stately piles. Stonehenge, for example, is now roped off and you can't climb on the stones; in Westminster Abbey the number of tourists is wearing down the flagstones; in Pisa the leaning tower leans at a greater angle every year and Venice, we're told, is in imminent danger of collapsing into the canals. What we need, if you ask me, is seven new wonders of the world, but *what* would qualify. Certainly the only Australian building to get a guernsey in that sort of list would be the Opera House. Then I suppose there's the Eiffel Tower, Disneyland, the World Trade Building in New York. All a bit boring though, aren't they?

The thing is they don't make Seven Wonders of the World like they used to. Just take the Pyramids, built 2000 years before Christ and still standing. Some of the other wonders, unfortunately, didn't do too well. The Hanging Gardens of Babylon stopped hanging and fell down around 600 BC. The statue of Zeus at Olympia, 30 feet high, plated with gold and ivory and showing the god on an ornate throne, was destroyed in the 5th century AD. Then there was the Temple of Artemis at Ephesus, built by that rich bloke Croesus—that was destroyed by the Goths in 262 AD.

I'd have loved to have done a bit of rubber-necking at the Mausoleum of Halicarnassus, the world's first mausoleum built for a bloke called—wait for it—Mausolus. Bits of it still survive in the British Museum. Then there was the Colossus of Rhodes, an iron reinforced bronze statue 100 feet high, built in honour of the Sun God. That stood in the harbour in Rhodes but there's no way it could have straddled it, despite what Shakespeare said. The Colossus fell down during an earthquake in 653 AD and was apparently broken up and flogged off in bits by the Arabs.

It seems to me that most of the Egyptian wonders of the world had that enduring quality. Apart from the Pyramids, there was the Lighthouse of Pharos of Alexandria which endured as late as the time of Robin Hood.

I'm often haunted by that final scene in the movie *Planet of the Apes*, when Charlton Heston rides out along the deserted beach to find the remains of the Statue of Liberty. I'm just wondering how many of our Australian landmarks would survive for 4000 years like the Pyramids. Would the sun still be glinting on those glazed tiles at the Opera House? Will the North Shore trains still go rattling over the Bridge? Somehow I doubt that even these two most celebrated tourist attractions will make it into the 22nd century.

No, there is probably only one Australian wonder that will make it, that is if it hasn't been worn down by all those sandshoes, and that's Ayers Rock. Like the man said, they don't build them like that anymore.

Vietnam blues

For about five years now, Vietnam has been back on the tourist map. Not that Hanoi is about to become the Cannes of South East Asia. The Wollongong perhaps. However, to anyone who is interested in world politics or simply the aftermath of forty years of war, Vietnam is required viewing. ABC cameraman Johnnie Hagan went there with a party accompanying the Minister for Foreign Affairs, Bill Hayden.

Johnnie Hagan is an experienced cameraman well used to dodging bullets, but the main hazard he encountered in Hanoi was the erratic nature of the power supply. Checking into his hotel he switched on the lights and the ceiling fan, but nothing happened. Being a pragmatist, John decided that the best thing to do was to go out, have a few drinks and dinner and then reconsider the situation.

It was a hot night and the absence of the ceiling fan made sleep difficult. 'I lay down on top of the bed with nothing on,' he recalled. At three in the morning, the power supply was suddenly restored. John awoke to find the ceiling fan roaring around at full speed like the propellers on an East West Airlines Fokker Friendship. 'I wasn't so much worried about being woken up,' said John, 'but I felt that my private parts were in grave danger should the blades become disconnected from the fan.'

The Australian Trade Union delegation who checked into

another hotel in Hanoi also had some problems. While shaving, one of the delegates rested his elbows on the wash basin and it wrenched itself from the wall and deluged the entire room.

Visiting politicians and trade unionists apart, I'm told the Russians are the most visible of the tourist groups in Hanoi these days. At Vung Tau, where once Australian servicemen disported themselves in the surf, it is now possible to see Russian matrons sitting under what at first glance look like sun umbrellas, but in actual fact are war surplus American parachutes. Australian servicemen who were at Vung Tau might remember the bar named after the VC winner, Peter Badco. You can't get Fosters or Fourex there anymore, just a type of Vietnamese vodka which tastes like dieseline. The Russians too have left their mark on Vietnamese cuisine. In addition to satays and chicken with lemon grass, you'll these days be offered dumplings, chicken Kiev and beetroot soup, which are all right in the Gulag Archipelago but not very practical if it's 90° in the shade. However, every Vietnamese menu has a silver lining. Thanks to years of French rule, French wines and champagnes are plentiful, cheap and largely ignored by the Vietnamese.

Vietnam probably won't be a prime tourist spot for some years. There are no discos, except the one at the Billabong Club in the Australian Embassy in Hanoi. There are no rental cars, no casinos and even Saigon's famous hookers have now been subjected to a re-education programme and are working in the fields as labourers.

As far as tourist attractions are concerned there are some beautiful Buddhist pagodas and many lovely colonial buildings that were unaffected by the bombing of North Vietnam. The United States dropped 100 000 tonnes of bombs on Vietnam and if you are interested in knowing their type, size and killing power you can see them all in the revolutionary museum in Hanoi.

One of the most frequently asked questions on 'Traveller's Tales' is 'What's the beer like over there?' I am reliably informed that the beer in Hanoi is like formalin but the beer in the south, which is called *Barmi* is quite drinkable.

The narrow boats

Wasn't it Ratty who said there was nothing nicer than messing about in boats? I would like to improve on that slightly and say that there's nothing nicer than messing about in narrow boats, or what the uninitiated refer to as barges.

In the middle of England, between the suave south and the sturdy north, there's the unlovely Black Country. The area could not be more appropriately name—the cradle of the British industrial revolution—it certainly has its share of dark satanic mills. In fact, it is said that when Queen Victoria was travelling north from London by train she ordered that the carriage blinds be drawn because she couldn't bear to look at the place.

Geographically, the Black Country is north west of Birmingham and is bordered by towns like Wolverhampton, Dudley, Coseley, Tipton and Smethwick. While it may have declined in importance industrially, it is now becoming known as the Venice of England. And it is virtually the crossroads for England's inland waterways system. It is possible to hire one of those lovely narrow boats and go puttering along the canal system for about $50 a day, but then the boats will sleep six people, so it's cheaper if you go with a crowd.

And what a civilised way to travel. The boats usually have those big one-cyclinder coal or wood burning engines that push you along at about one mile an hour. I know it's difficult to believe, but it really is a whole different world looking at industrial Britain from a barge. The various preservation societies have done a lot to clear the canals of weed and renovate the buildings alongside. There is a long tunnel at Dudley, which you navigate by lying on your back on the boat with your feet on the roof and pushing yourself through. Then there are always the locks to navigate. Don't forget that the levels through the Black Country vary enormously. Most of the lock gates aren't manned so it is up to you to pump the water through and close the gates.

And what about the locals? Well, they are usually short, dark, worried little men with not much forehead and eyebrows too close together. They are very big on pigeons and their idea of a bit of fun is to spend Saturday afternoon catching rats on the canal towpath, usually with dogs. The dogs are a bit like the people. The favourite breed is the Staffordshire bull terrier: stubborn, deep-chested and vicious in a scrap; in the 19th century they used to use them for that particularly cruel sport known as bull baiting.

As for the landscape, well it's a bit like the surface of the moon, full of what the locals call toccy bonks or pit mounds. You might go into a pub and find that the whole place is leaning at a crazy angle because of the subsidence caused by mining underneath. Some of the canals join up with the English rivers and if you have the time, you can get as far as the sea. All in all, it's a gentle, relaxing sort of trip, a very different sort of holiday and there is nothing quite like it in Australia. As the locals say: 'Yo can 'ave a lot of fun up the cut.'

Speaking da lingo

THE virtues of not learning the language when visiting a foreign country have been discussed many times. But what about the prospect of learning an international language which is so widely used that people have to get together at a conference each year to talk it.

I am talking about Esperanto. Esperanto is a tiny principality sandwiched between Liechtenstein and Wolverhampton. It is so inaccessible as to be not really worth visiting. A peculiar custom of the Esperantise is always to remember to shake hands with everybody when entering a railway carriage.

All this, of course, is absolute nonsense. Anybody will tell you that Esperanto was invented about 100 years ago by an eye doctor called Zamenhof. It sounds a bit like a mixture of German, Italian and English; it has an alphabet of 28 letters and is strictly phonetic.

It has, in fact, been a partial success. Warsaw, Peking, the Vatican, Rome and Belgrade occasionally put out broadcasts in Esperanto and the Pope is said to be sympathetic to it, but then he is a multilingual chap.

The Esperanto headquarters are in London and they were parodied in a Graham Greene novel called *The Confidential Agent*. It is true to say that a certain air of dedicated crankiness hangs about the place.

The language was designed to increase international understanding and prevent war. But since nations get on best when they studiously avoid one another, its failure is both honourable and predictable. Still, apart from that, it is supposed to be five times easier to learn than French. In Switzerland a weekly news magazine is published, not to promote the language but to demonstrate its practicality. In Holland they put it in telephone kiosks and it's used for railway timetables in Denmark, Italy, Yugoslavia and, of course, Poland where it was invented.

The notion that if only nation could speak unto nation is ineradicable and deeply idealistic. In fact we're as nationalistic as ever about languages. Giscard D'Estaing was said to be very peeved about the spread of Anglicised French—called Franglais.

A few years ago an enterprising Belgian even published a book on how to swear in Esperanto. But frankly, who'd change 'bastard' to its equivalent in Esperanto—'fraulinido', or what about 'kondamninda', which means 'damn'.

No, I think I'll stick to raising my voice, speaking very clearly and using hand signals.

Love at first bite

BELIEVE it or not there are now Dracula tours to Romania, tours that take in the castle of Vladimir Dracul, the impaler. We haven't been able to establish whether you can book them in Australia, although you certainly can in London.

However, there is an agent in Australia for Carpati, the National Tourist Office of Romania. This operates rather like the Russian Intourist agency and it is advisable to make all your arrangements with them. Otherwise, if you drive into Romania unannounced, you will probably be asked to part with a large amount of money at the border which has to be changed into the local currency of *leis* and *banis* and then will not be changed back.

It isn't an expensive country. Hotels range from $20—$45 a night and that includes breakfast, but—and this is a big but—the season is very short: from 16 June to 30 September. If you go either side of that a lot of hotels may be closed. I heard the story of one Australian tourist who went to a roadside restaurant in the off season. He was given a 28-page menu, but everything was off except the Chicken Kiev. He said that the people generally were rude and sullen and if he never saw Romania again it would be too soon, but then that's his opinion.

If you do go to Romania and knock someone down in your car, be prepared to be detained in the country until your case comes up which might be three months. Still, if you need to raise the cash for your accommodation you can always sell your jeans and your chewing gum.

Tutti Frutti

I can never understand why people get excited about Sweden. Ever since I can remember, Sweden has always been held up as a model of what all other countries should strive to achieve. It is true that Sweden is an enlightened democracy and was the first country to introduce abortion on demand and homosexual law reform. But what a very dull lot they are. I'm told that behind that blank, formal and meticulous exterior there lurks the genuine romantic. My experience is you have to peel off a good many layers before you get to it. I would now like to introduce you to a sound you will hear a lot in Sweden.

Yes folks, that gap in the text indicates a long Nordic silence and anyone who has seen an Ingmar Bergman film will know that Sweden is full of them. There seems to be an awful lot of standing around looking gloomy.

Before long, of course, someone is bound to trot out that old chestnut about the Swedes having the highest suicide rate in the world. Well, about 19 people per 1000 do themselves in every year and most of them are men, but that still puts Sweden well behind the Viennese and some states in the USA. But the reason so many men commit suicide is perfectly obvious. There are no pubs in Sweden. Can you imagine it? There are bars in the big cities and the hotels, but no pubs as we know them.

Drinking tends to be done in the home because the penalties for drink driving are very severe. And the young are actively discouraged from drinking too. Outside the equivalent of a Swedish grog shop I was approached by a teenager who offered me kroner to buy him a bottle of Scotch. It's OK for tourists, but not for kids.

But when the Swedes do let their hair down they really go over the top. This is best observed on the ferry which runs between Halsingborg in Sweden and Helsingor in Denmark. The ferry takes only about fifteen minutes to cross the water between the two countries, and it is usually full of Swedish businessmen. On the ferry you can drink all day if you want to, so businessmen tend to conclude their affairs quickly and then spend the rest of the day going backwards and forwards between the two countries, getting well and truly Adrian Quist. The day I travelled on that ferry the whole boat was awash with vomit.

I remember once having a real fun night in a place called Vaxjo in central Sweden. Because there were no pubs I sat in a coffee bar, drank five cups of coffee and then went to see a fifth-rate Jerry Lewis movie with Swedish subtitles. The whole town closed at half past nine and as I left the cinema they were turning off the lights.

Drinking habits even in the home tend to be furtive. There's a lot of hiding the bottle from the wife or the mother-in-law, and one in every ten males is a problem drinker.

Mother-in-law jokes, in fact jokes told generally about women, are very popular in Sweden. Sample: The best way of getting rid of a noise in your car is to let her drive.

Swedish men are not only henpecked but outnumbered by women; this probably accounts for the fact that they very rarely give up their seats to women in trains or stand aside to let the fair sex out of elevators. All this seems to conjure up a picture of too few men being chased by packs of snake-hipped Swedish blondes. But if Sweden is a sexual smorgasbord, why are the Swedes so dedicatedly gloomy about it all?

There is no earthly point in learning the lingo in Sweden because it defies comprehension and is full of Os with crosses through them or other letters festooned with growths. To the uninitiated, Swedish sounds like someone blowing into a stone hot water bottle. In reality, manÿ Swedish words are the same as English; for example, arm, hand, man, son and finger are exactly the same. However one can pretend to speak Swedish by using the all-purpose 'Scandiwegian' phrase: 'Tutti frutti, athletes foot'. It has to be said on a high, fluty Swedish voice, like this: 'Toota-fluta-at-alayta-foota'. See what I mean? Don't forget to use it next time you are trying to buy a drink in Stockholm. After all, there's no place like Stockholm.

Jets

FLYING the Atlantic by Concorde has to be the only way to go. The Concorde is small inside, more like the inside of a Fokker Friendship than a Jumbo. Compared to a Jumbo, it's like a sports car. It can cross the Atlantic both ways in less time than it takes a Jumbo to make a one-way crossing. Everybody has been knocking the Concorde for years but it is still the best looking plane in the sky, and I'm pleased to report that at the time of writing, the big white bird is starting to make a modest profit for the two airlines who operate it, British Airways and Air France.

Concorde is the only plane capable of maintaining twice the speed of sound for three hours or more. There are military aircraft that can do it, but they guzzle fuel like it's going out of fashion, and have to slow down from time to time to take on fuel from airborne tankers.

Concorde is the only supersonic airliner in regular scheduled service, discounting the Russian TU 144 'Concordski'. The Concordski was a straight pinch of the Concorde design, right down to its 'droop snoot' and slender delta wing. But a disastrous crash at the Paris Air Show a few years back put paid to the TU-144's chances of ever becoming a rival to the Anglo-French marvel. The TU-144 was introduced on a high speed mail service from one end of the Soviet Union to the other. The *Time* Magazine correspondent who managed to get a free seat on its inaugural flight was mortified to find that the passenger aisles were filled with passengers' baggage and cardboard boxes containing newspapers. The 'Concordski' took off at such a steep angle that most of the cargo slid down to the back of the plane and lay there in a heap.

Back in 1962, the Americans also had a rival to the Concorde. Built by Boeing it was designed to fly at three times the speed of sound and carry 200 passengers from New York to London in three hours (Concorde does it in under four, but has made the journey in three hours, sixteen minutes). The Boeing 2707, as it was called, never got off the ground, although developing the mock-up cost more than a real Concorde.

The cost of developing a plane to go even faster than Concorde was astronomical. Concorde is built largely of aluminium. To go any faster than Mach 2 requires the plane to be built of fancy metals which will withstand the high temperatures. The Boeing 2707 was to be built of titanium and stainless steel. At any event, Boeing decided they couldn't afford to build the plane without money from the government, and by a very narrow vote in the Senate, the 2707 was stillborn. The huge mock-up, nearly 200 feet long, languished in Seattle for a while with its huge tail poking out from the hangar. Then it went up for sale as a fairground attraction. In some ways the 2707 was a freak of nature. For a start it only had one wing; that is one half of the huge delta wing. The plane was virtually a shell; there were phoney paper instruments inside and precious little else. On the slender 'droop snoot' were displayed the logos of all the airlines that had placed options on the aircraft.

When I finally ran the 2707 down it was inside an old corrugated iron shed at a place called Kissimee in Florida. Someone had bought it as a static exhibit but had run out of money. The Florida Tourist Bureau (to whom I am eternally indebted) were flattered that a television crew from Australia had come 19 000 kilometres to film this rusting piece of scrap. The great white whale was now up for grabs to anyone who wanted to buy her, although what one would do with an unused supersonic airliner is anybody's guess.

The asking price was $US300 000 which seemed awfully expensive to me considering that the thing wouldn't even FLY.

However, that's the going price for titanium these days, which, incidentally, is made from sand mined from the beaches of Queensland.

Some weeks later, I managed to get a ride on Concorde from Washington to London. We had been waiting at Cape Canaveral for the second launch of the Space Shuttle, which as usual was delayed because of a technical hitch. The options were either to stay around to watch the shuttle or to ride to London on the SST. We chose the SST. Unfortunately, the changing temperatures were playing merry hell with my physiology, and I rode supersonic to London with a temperature of 100° and a burning fever.

The people I feel sorry for on Concorde are the cabin crew. The single aisle is so narrow that there is no room for a passenger to get past the drinks trolley while the crew are serving refreshments. Not only that, Concorde flies slightly nose up which means that the crew have to push the trolley uphill. Add to that the debilitating effects of flying at high altitude (Concorde flies twice as high as anything else—nearly 20 kilometres up) means that the crews get very tired.

Travelling on the flight deck of Concorde is extraordinary. As Captain Monty Burton explained, the windows of the plane become hotter in flight. Outside, the skin of the aircraft becomes hot enough to fry eggs on. And strange to tell, the whole plane becomes ten inches longer as the metal expands in flight. The flight engineer mentioned how he was in the habit of wedging his flight manual between the narrow gap in between the instrument panels. But the gap was only there while the plane was going supersonic. When he arrived in London, it had contracted again and the flight manual was well and truly stuck there.

Concorde is not allowed to go supersonic over land because it leaves a supersonic boom in its wake. I have heard supersonic booms made by a variety of aircraft and at various altitudes and think the noise level is greatly exaggerated.

Even when it is throttled back, Concorde can still fly right up to the sound barrier, which makes it about 160 kilometres an hour faster than all subsonic transport planes. However, even at twice the speed of sound there is no sensation of speed. At Concorde's cruising altitude over the Atlantic the sky gores from blue to dark purple. The stars seem very bright, almost as if you could touch them. When the ocean is not obscured by clouds you can see the curvature of the earth. But the view from the window is usually disappointing, like most jets, and Concorde's windows are only half the size of those on a 747.

Windows are always a problem for aircraft designers. Obviously anything with holes or perforation is going to be a weaker structure and at one stage it was considered that Concorde would have no passenger windows at all. But the psychological effects of being trapped inside an aluminium tube and not being able to see out would be considerable. Finally, Concorde's fuselage sides were hewn out of billets of aluminium four inches thick...and there were windows in them too.

Concorde's passengers have always been decidely up market: film stars, politicians and heads of state. Sad to say, Henry Kissinger wasn't on the flight when we boarded at Washington, neither was Bianca Jagger or Rod Stewart. Still, maybe next time. The Concorde is no longer a new plane, but it will probably still be in service ten years from now because it is only in the air for three hours a day. It's technology is dated compared with more modern, conventional planes and its systems are difficult to maintain. But somehow I get the impression that British Airways and Air France will be getting their money's worth out of Concorde. That familiar triangle in the sky is going to be around for quite a while yet.

Brussel sprouts, please

THE first thing you notice about the Belgians is that they are very big on shaking hands. Why we shake hands at all, of course, is supposed to date back to Roman times. Obviously if you have the other person's mitt in yours he cannot be hiding a knife in it, and I guess the Belgians have been invaded so many times that they now choose their friends very carefully. In fact it used to be rather difficult to get to know the Belgians. Young people might be engaged to one another for quite long periods without ever being invited home; in fact many Belgian houses have those slatted shutters which give the impression that no one actually lives there at all. No, the reason they are closed is that Belgians have a horror of draughts—you usually find windows firmly shut and offices, homes and restaurants over-heated.

Belgium isn't France and it isn't Holland, although they speak both French and Flemish. The national drink is beer, rather than wine, and they are crazy about chips. In fact, if you associate places with smells you will know that the morning smell in Brussels is coffee and the evening smell is potato chips, eaten in great quantities and usually with mayonnaise. As for coffee, the Belgians drink it until it's coming out of their ears, and children drink it from about the time they can walk.

The Belgians are nuts about sport and, most of all of course, cycling. Every Belgian hopes to win the Tour de France. One

117

man I know once saw two nuns on a tandem pedalling across a golf course during a snowstorm. And they are especially fond of soccer and pelote, which is a cross between tennis, handball... and pigeon racing. They are also into cock-fighting, although they never quite got round to making it legal. I, for one, am grateful for that. Nasty vicious business.

Like the British, the Belgians are a nation of shopkeepers and the shops stay open till all hours. It is possible to buy a pair of shoes at half past one in the morning, I know someone who actually did this but she fell asleep while trying them on and only later realised they were two sizes too big. Imagine being shoe-horned into a pair of brogues while snoring your head off!

But above all, the Belgians have their priorities right. To the German it's work; to the French it's love; but to the Belgian the most important thing is food. They like to eat meat once a day and call it a beefsteak, whether it is or not. In fact, when Belgians are looking after their interests they're looking after their beefsteak, not to mention their Brussels sprouts, grown since the 13th century and still going strong.

You can drive from one end of Belgium to the other in half a day, but don't pass it up. It's got rather more to offer than just Brussels sprouts.

Mao's tomb

WHEN Sandy and Carol arrived in China's capital, Beijing, they were excited at the prospect of eight days in which to experience China. With a map and guide book in hand, they caught a taxi to Tiananmen Square, regarded as the city centre. This square, bordered by Mao's memorial—The Great Hall of the People, the Historical Museum and the Tianamen Gate—is capable of holding 500 000 people and on any one day there will be tens of thousands milling around the halls, queueing to see Mao's embalmed body or to have their photos taken at Tiananmen Gate with Mao's picture behind.

Although Carol and Sandy weren't interested in having their photograph taken, they were fascinated by the equipment the Chinese tourists were using. There were a dozen large cans, something like old-fashioned tin ice-cream containers, and these were perched on legs with enormous protruding lenses on the front. The up-market cameras used by Chinese tourists are box brownies—photography is obviously becoming a serious business in contemporary China.

Monday is one of the three days when Mao's tomb opens to the public and if you join a tour for western tourists, the guide will interrupt the long queue of Chinese and you can then virtually push your way in! Some Australians find this approach rather embarrassing. Cameras and bags are not permitted in the tomb and if you are with a tour you simply leave all personal belongings on the bus and the driver keeps an eye on them.

But if you go alone there is an easy and exciting approach. 'You have to check your bags and cameras in at one of the six roadside stalls,' explained Sandy. 'You exchange your goods for a token to use for collection later, which sounds simple enough but there are at least 100 people at each small stall, all wanting to be first. Remarkably, we each received a tin token and so we joined the queue of Chinese.'

The Chinese are being actively encouraged to travel around their own country and at any tourist venue there are thousands of Chinese as eager as their overseas counterparts to see the points of interest.

'I know China's a land of over a billion people but I didn't expect most of them to be lining up to see Mao,' exclaimed Carol. 'Without a hint of exaggeration the queue was at least five people wide and a kilometre long, and 95 per cent of the Chinese were in either blue, khaki or grey Mao suits.

We all know that the Chinese have glossy black hair and in Beijing the clothing is very drab and colourless except, that is, for the tiny children who are dressed in iridescent pinks and greens. So for Sandy and Carol, both with very blonde hair and sporting bright yellow windcheaters, it wasn't easy to look inconspicuous. But there was no time to worry as the queue started moving at a rapid rate. The entrance to Mao's Memorial was roped off and every couple of minutes about 400 people were released to enter.

'As soon as the man with the megaphone told us to start moving, everyone marched towards the entrance, did a sharp left-hand turn and walked briskly up the steps past the sign which said "No Stopping and No Talking",' said Sandy. 'Carol and I had to run a little just to keep pace, and when we entered the hall containing Mao's embalmed body in a glass case, we had to keep moving through and straight out the exit.'

Mao's case is about 4 metres from where you are allowed to walk but there is no time to stop and study the figure. 'Before we knew it we were out on the other side, queueing for our bags and cameras,' explained Carol and Sandy. 'We'd removed our passports and wallets but there was no need as string was used to tie our possessions into one bundle. In fact, the entire time we were scouting about the highlights of Beijing such as the Great Wall, the Underground City, the Ming Tombs and the unforgettable Forbidden City, or simply walking the streets, neither of us felt any animosity or any need to worry about the safety of the possessions we were carrying.'

Tourism is expanding at an incredible rate in China. New hotels are being built to try and accommodate the influx. Thousands of people are attending hotel management and tour guide courses. Of course all this will change the face of China. Even now it is impossible to be sure that something happening today will occur in the same or even similar way next month. But Sandy and Carol are glad to have seen part of China in early 1985 and although their eight days were full of marvels and surprises, their most memorable event was Mao's tomb. 'It's partly because it was our first day and we were excited and wide-eyed at being among a new culture, but mainly that we'd broken convention and as individuals joined the Chinese and done exactly as they had. The lack of special privileges resulted in very special memories.'

Whingeing Poms

ONE of the main accusations levelled at the English in Australia is that they are always whingeing about something, and the answer to that, I suppose, is you have to complain or you don't get anything done. However, in my experience most Australians don't complain enough, particularly when they are on holiday and especially in restaurants or hotels. And it gets even worse when they are overseas. The same macho bronzed Anzac who lords it around the beach in his own country is likely to be reduced to blubbering jelly by the first hotel desk clerk in Torremolinos. If you are buying a second hand car you wouldn't dream of not taking it for a test drive, but most people are prepared to fork out 50 bucks a night for a hotel room without even checking it out first.

Always check out your room: count the coathangers, inspect the bath and that little overflow slot in the washbasin—if it is clean then the room's probably going to be OK. Check the shower, the curtains and the bedside lighting and if the room isn't suitable don't be afraid to say so and ask to see another. The hotel business is a service industry and you expect service. And if the attitude is, 'Don't ask me mate. I only work here,' ask to see someone in authority. Many people don't even establish how much the room is going to cost for the night and then complain when they get the bill.

Then there is the question of how you behave with hotel

staff. Why is it that even the most assertive company director becomes meek and servile when checking into a hotel...I'll tell you why, it's because he is not on his own territory and he feels ill at ease and a bit lost.

There is no need to lord it over people, just be fair, frank and open. I once saw a well known Australian film critic attempting to pull rank on a foreign airline employee by using that dreadful phrase, 'Don't you know who I am?' 'No sir,' said the man very civilly, 'I'm afraid I don't.' The film critic pressed the point. 'How long have you worked here?' 'Well sir,' said the clerk, 'I've worked here long enough to know all the important people.'

Then we come to the vexing question of tipping. I know you are not necessarily expected to tip in Australia, but in many countries like the States you are and there is no getting away from it. But don't overtip. Fifty cents a suitcase is quite enough. And never make the mistake of asking a porter 'How much should I tip you?' It's embarrassing to him and it shows him that you don't really know what you're doing. The Aga Khan's trick was to tip very heavily when he arrived at a hotel and hardly at all when he left—that way he was sure of good service.

Jamaica, man

NOT long after Christopher Columbus came back from Jamaica, Queen Isabella of Spain asked him what it was like. He crumpled up a piece of paper and said, 'It looks like that, your Majesty.' And it is a bit like crumpled paper: mountainous in the centre with four peaks over 6000 feet, curving downwards to white sand beaches and waving palms.

There are no true Jamaicans any more; when the Spaniards arrived there were Indians but the conquistadors wiped them out to a man. The Jamaicans today are the descendants of the Africans taken over for slavery. Generally they're a pretty easy going lot; sometimes they are sullen and sometimes they flare up, but they are rarely malicious.

It is one of the few places in the world where women outnumber men. Lovemaking is cheap, but contraception is expensive and many villages still have no electricity...so what else can you sensibly do in the dark. Jamaicans aren't big on marriage either. For a start it's expensive, man, and even to get married after ten years of living together is regarded as a mad reckless rush.

Jamaica is only 140 miles long and you can drive from one end to the other in four hours. If you fly there you land at one of the two international airports, Kingston or Monego Bay, which the locals call 'Mo' Bay. Incidentally, Air Jamaica is one of the few airlines I've been on which had fashion modelling in flight.

Jamaica is the home of Reggae music and the Rastafarian movement. The Rastas are rather fierce looking men who claim to be directly descended from the late Emperor Haile Selassie of Ethiopia. They also pong a bit because to make their hair stand up in weird shapes they smear animal dung on it. The all take it terribly seriously and are in favour of being repatriated to Ethiopia, but now that Haile Selassie has tumbled off the twig and Ethiopia's a Marxist state, there isn't much hope of that. Haile Selassie did once pay a visit to Jamaica although of the three African heads of state arriving at the airport one was found to be Haile Selassie, one was fairly Selassie and one wasn't Selassie at all.

Eating and drinking can be quite exciting in Jamaica—curried goat and rice, pepperpot soup and roast suckling pig, washed down with Red Stripe beer or, of course, Jamaica Rum. After that if you fancy a fling you can always do a turn at the local pocomania meetings. These are wild dances where the participants tend to fall down in a trance. We call it disco, I think. And if you are really in amongst the high rollers, how about a week at what's reckoned to be most expensive hotel in the world; Frenchman's Cove. It will cost you about $1000 a week and for that you get all meals, drinks, entertainment—even the long distance phone calls are free. So if you are after a Dreadlock Holiday, Jamaica's the place. But go easy on the pocomania.

The loneliest island in the world

Do you remember a few years ago when they sold wool in skeins? You know, those long loops of wool...Mum used to ask Dad to stick his hands out and would then wind the wool round them into a ball. In England my Dad had a family business which teetered on the brink of bankruptcy until, in the white heat of reborn British technology, he invented the Watson Easyway Patented Woolwinder.

The Easyway Patented Woolwinder had three arms like a helicopter rotor and a knurled knob with which to clamp it to the table. You put the skein around the arms and wound the wool onto a ball. It was probably our most dynamic invention, apart from the cast ornaments for Maori coffins which were all exported to New Zealand. Anyway we sold thousands of woolwinders in their hideous green boxes. Every home had one. They sold for six shillings and eleven pence and were hailed as a major technological breakthrough, until some smart Chinaman in Hong Kong brought out a plastic version which sold for one shilling and eleven pence. Then the wool companies started selling wool already in balls and what had been a major breakthrough suddenly became six shillings and eleven pence worth of chromium-plated scrap. We were stuck with hundreds of the things.

So what has all this to do with travel, I hear you cry. Well, it was quite obvious that the only place to sell our woolwinders

was Tristan da Cunha. I hadn't actually heard of Tristan da Cunha until then. It is known as the loneliest island in the world, stuck in the South Atlantic about 1000 miles off Africa. There it was in my stamp album. Tristan da Cunha's industries are fishing and wool. So in a major export drive we managed to sell two dozen woolwinders to Tristan da Cunha. Well, there can't be much to do there, why else would the poor blighters want an easy-to-assemble, chromium-plated device with knurled knob and attachments? Anyway with rising disbelief we packaged up half a dozen and posted them off. There was only about one ship a year so it took months for the cheque to come back with, wait for it, an order for another dozen woolwinders. In my imagination I saw the sturdy little islanders cheerfully assembling their woolwinders with their faces glowing in anticipation of many hours' woolwinding.

Then suddenly Tristan da Cunha was in the news. The volcano on the island blew up and all the islanders were evacuated to Britain. Just imagine: as the lava and ash rained down, which possessions would *you* reach for? Certainly your bankbook and your jewellery case. But probably not your Easyway Patented Woolwinder with knurled knob and attachments.

I don't suppose I shall ever get to Tristan da Cunha. I don't even know whether the islanders ever went back there. But perhaps when the archaeologists are chipping away at the lava in 1000 years time they will find in the dust a strange, chromium-plated device with a knurled knob in a hideous green box, costing six shillings and eleven pence.

Run

Half an hour's drive from the centre of Hong Kong is Repulse Bay, home of one of the most prolific movie studios in the world, run by the enigmatic Sir Run Run Shaw. This dignified Chinaman is to the movie industry what Henry Ford was to the motor car industry. He can make any sort of movie, so long as it's Kung Fu. For some years now he has been the world's leading maker and distributor of martial arts films, and his products are seen all over Asia.

Sir Run Run Shaw is one of two brothers who started their movie careers in Singapore (the other brother is Run Me Shaw). It was a Sunday when I visited the Shaw movie studios, but even so it was business as usual. A film was in production on the sound stage and the car park was full. Outside Sir Run Run's office a Rolls Royce was lording it over a lowly Datsun. Inside, Sir Run Run extended a dry palm and asked me to sit down.

In Hollywood a film might be in production for three years from script approval to final cut. How long was a Shaw film in production? He smiled. 'We usually complete a film in one month from the moment the script is approved to the final editing. If it goes any longer than this, then I ask questions,' he said.

The Shaw Brothers movie house is in production seven days a week, but he never has any trouble with the unions. There aren't any. 'People in Hong Kong are glad to have a job,' he said. 'I think perhaps people work harder here than in your country.' There were signs, I said, that the Kung Fu cult was petering out. Could he turn his talents to making other sorts of films? 'Of course,' he said. 'We are working on a romantic film. I'm afraid I cannot tell you much about it.'

And what did Sir Run Run think of the current wave of Australian films? 'I have seen some of them and they are very good.' Which one had he seen? 'I think it was called *Picnic at Hanging Lock*,' he said.

The ghost squadron

Down in southern Texas, near the Mexican border, a highly improbable bunch of characters has assembled the biggest private airforce in the world. This is the Confederate Airforce Ghost Squadron—a group of aviation enthusiasts dedicated to preserving the piston-engined planes or World War Two.

The place is called Harlingen in the heart of redneck country. It's a flat, fairly uninteresting piece of real estate and the Confederate Airforce is the only reason for going there. Certainly very few Australians would find the beaches of the Gulf of Mexico a patch on those back home. Add to that the clapboard weekenders, the restaurants selling Tex-Mex food and the rusting car bodies, and you have the picture. It was certainly a rusting car body we picked up at the airport. All the major car rental companies had rented out their stock for the entire week. I ended up with an '82 Dodge with faulty air conditioning and a rusting roof. Still it was only $15 a day.

It is the planes that people come to see at Harlingen. Every year thousands of air enthusiasts come from all over the world to gaze in wonder at Fifi, the B29 Superfortress, or the Heinkel bomber, or the immaculate US Navy Corsairs, or any one of a 30 other propeller driven planes.

Everything about the Confederate Airforce is pure 1940s nostalgia. The noses of the planes are covered with the Varga pin-up girls; Glenn Miller's band blares from every loud-

131

speaker; the hats and flying overalls are festooned with badges. This is a show for anyone who ever read *Biggles*.

But this is no static museum. All the planes fly and fly very well. It takes thousands of loving hours' work on the ground to keep them in the air. Some of the aircraft may look familiar, and they should. The Grumman Avengers were used in the opening titles of *Close Encounters of the Third Kind*; the Super-fortress starred in *The Right Stuff*; the Spitfire in *The Battle of Britain* and the B25s in *Catch 22*. The planes are so expensive to run that Hollywood often puts up the cash to keep them flying.

Where do you find pilots to fly planes that are 30−40 years old? Many of the colonels in the Confederate Airforce flew the aircraft in World War Two and they have passed on their expertise to younger pilots. There are no other ranks but colonel in the Confederate Airforce. Everybody is a colonel.

Surely the buck must stop somewhere? Well, theoretically it stops at the desk of Colonel Jethro Culpepper, a southern 'gennlemun' with curly a white moustache who looks like he could be related to the Colonel Sanders of fried chicken fame. I could not find anyone who had actually met Jethro but I was shown the private mint patch for the colonel's own mint juleps. Critics of the CAF say that it is a colossal waste of time and gasoline. Nowhere is that more obvious than in the re-enactment of the famous air battles of World War Two. The Zeros dive again to recreate the Battle for Midway, the bomber raids over Germany and the Battle of Britain. The highlight in this orgy of destruction is when the B29 flies over and pretends to drop the A−bomb on Hiroshima. Until quite recently they used to explode a device on the airfield to simulate the atomic mush-room. Then the stunt was dropped in the interests of good taste.

It's all good gung-ho stuff: the rattle of the machine guns, the whine of the props, the smoke and the flame. Many of the old colonels flew the aircraft in real combat situations, although most of them are getting a little long in the tooth. Colonel Carter McGregor used to fly B29s from bases in India to attack the Japanese mainland. What was it like flying a B29 again after forty years? 'Like takin' an alcoholic to a bar. Or like an old love affair,' he said. 'We aren't really glorifying war. What we're making people aware of is the contribution made by these planes. I hope it never happens again.'

It won't be possible to keep the planes flying forever. Sooner or later they will all end up as museum exhibits, since the spare parts are becoming more and more difficult to find. I hope they manage to keep some of them flying; there's certainly no other reason to visit unlovely Harlingen.

Swimming with the sharks

I F you have always wanted to go cruising but suspected it may be too boring, then the Lindblad Explorer is for you. It's a very special cruiser with a double reinforced hull, a bow thruster which allows incredible manoeuvrability and it can penetrate the most inaccessible corners of the globe. In fact it is an ice working vessel rather than an ice breaker and is best known for its voyages to the Arctic and the Antarctic. The ship is equipped with specially designed rubber boats called zodiacs which extend the limits of exploration so that passengers, fourteen at a time in each, can go into inlets, over coral reefs and along inland rivers where the ship cannot go.

On board there is an atmosphere of learning, as each expedition is accompanied by a group of experts who show films and give lectures on such topics as bird life, tidal habits, history, geography, local culture and marine life. Ron and Valerie Taylor, the shark people, have been all over the world lecturing on sharks and various fish and instructing passengers in diving and snorkelling. With an amazing wealth of knowledge about sharks, and feeling very comfortable with them in Australian waters, the Taylors always try to russle up a few so that the passengers can observe their ways. On one trip to Heron Island they collected all the scraps from the resort's kitchen, loaded the passengers and garbage into the zodiacs, and proceeded to feed them (the scraps not the passengers!) to the huge ferocious sharks which inhabit the waters beyond the coral reef. All the zodiacs were in one spot and as the garbage was hurled over the sides, 40, 50, even 60 sharks frenzied. 'The water was boiling with hungry sharks,' enthused Valerie. 'The passengers absolutely loved it. We had to do it five times. And the poor cook had to drag meat out of the deep freeze to appease everyone.'

Another time, at Marion Reef, off the Queensland coast, every single passenger was snorkelling among 26 sharks, having been assured by Ron and Valerie that it was completely safe. Yes, safe, even though these sharks were territorial, potentially dangerous, and one of them had once bitten Valerie on the arm. That is indeed undying trust. But because these sharks had never been harmed by people they would, in turn, never inflict harm on people. 'As long as they are not provoked and remain unafraid,' added Valerie. Swimming with sharks was an experience that no passenger could ever forget and, yes, they all came out unscathed.

Shark investigation is still incredibly exciting for Valerie and she says that sharks are in her blood. But the ship and what the captain did with it was equally incredible. What stays in Valerie's mind most is when he put the nose of the Lindblad right up to an erupting volcano which was sticking out of the ocean. It was at night and all the red hot lava was pouring down into the sea. She could hear it crumbling and rumbling and splashing into the waves and could feel the tremendous heat. Everyone experienced it as they stood on deck staring at what can only be described as a miracle.

And that's the sort of thing that happens when you travel on this remarkable cruising ship. 'It's a great adventure in absolute luxury,' sighed Valerie. 'And the ship is just sitting there waiting for you.'

White water rafting in New Guinea

New Guinea, Australia's closest neighbour, still fails to attract tourists the way Fiji and Bali do. Many potential visitors believe they are taking their lives into their hands by venturing there and although there *is* the occasional border skirmish with Irian Jaya or the odd highland tribal fight, if you make certain areas off limits you will be safe.

New Guinea is full of intrigue: the beaches at Madang are as good as those at any resort, the accommodation is reasonable in terms of price and comfort and the scenery is outstanding. The land is dominated by a chain of lofty mountains and this terrain makes flying in local light aircraft fairly hazardous. However, I survived the flight from Port Moresby, the capital, through clouded mountain tops to Lae, with only one or two heart-stoppers on the way.

A group of adventurers was to meet at Lae to embark on a white water rafting trip down the Watut River. Almost immediately it was evident that this was a do-it-yourself holiday. Eight of us—six passengers and two oarsmen—began by loading the two heavy rubber rafts, a week's worth of food and water, and personal luggage, onto a ricketty old truck which was to transport us 50 kilometres to the 'put in' spot on the river. It seemed that no sooner had these chores been carried out than it was time to unload it all again, drag it to the river's edge and inflate the rafts for the 200 kilometres of white water rafting along the

Watut. A sprinkling of local natives helped us push the rafts into the river, which was completely calm at this point, and pushed us on our way.

It was a relief to be able to sit down, put up our tired feet, and be rowed along the river bordered by such lush, jungley vegetation. Passengers require no real skill for such a journey as the oarsmen do all the manoeuvring. All you have to do is to 'hit the high side' when the raft comes in contact with a rock or a vigorous rapid. At first the rapids were more like ripples on a lake until we rounded the first bend and within seconds we were almost freefalling down a four-metre waterfall. There were screams of excitement as the falls became bigger, better and more exhilarating and we all clung to the sides of the raft or to each other as we dived for the 'high side'.

There should have been ample room for the oarsman and three passengers in each raft, but Phil, a lobster catcher from northern New South Wales, was decidedly large. He must have weighed some 120 kilograms and taken up most of the available space but he was thoroughly enjoying being thrown around the raft—until we hit the largest rapid of all. The rafts swirled around in the suds and, before we knew it, Phil was part of this giant washing machine. We couldn't help visualising him being sucked under by the enormous force of this mighty river. 'Go with the flow and for God's sake try to keep your head above water,' yelled the oarsman. Fortunately Phil was a good swimmer but he was at the mercy of the gods as it would have been suicidal for any of us to jump in and attempt to help. Added to which, the other raft was downriver and oblivious to this drama.

It was then that a miracle happened. Some natives suddenly appeared on the bank and crawled along an almost horizontal tree trunk protruding into the water. They formed a human chain and hung a thick fishing net in Phil's path which immediately entangled him. Then he was dragged from man to man until safely ashore.

Once in calm water, the natives were waiting to escort us to Tiak, their local village. On arrival, we saw Phil, looking somewhat bedraggled but resolutely smiling as one of the elders held a glass of local hootch, a kind of whisky, to his lips. 'There was only a moment of panic,' said Phil. 'I was really starting to get the hang of it when my friends here interrupted.' Phil knew the people of Tiak couldn't speak English so he wasn't offending them. Our group leader, David, had lived in New Guinea on and off for ten years and was fluent in Pidgin but it didn't need words to see how happy the heroes were.

Tiak was a typical New Guinea village. All the buildings stood on stilts, dogs and pigs and chooks roamed freely and the kids, at least those who could keep their eyes off us, played the local version of football in the recreation area. The ground was covered in red saliva from the men and women who continually chewed betel nuts.

There was no tribal fighting in this region. They were so friendly that when we left, the entire village came to wave us off. Some of the men even ran along the banks to ensure that their newfound friend, Phil, would be 'all right, mate!'

South Africa

ONE o'clock in the morning is no time to make one's first acquaintance with a fully-grown African lioness, particularly when one has drunk a little too much South African port.

She stood in the glare from the headlights, yellow eyes unblinking. We must have looked an odd lot—a group of Aussie travel writers, slightly tipsy, doing what slightly tipsy travel writers do up against trucks. Ever so *sotto voce* our guide said, 'Make no sudden movements. Very quietly, get back into the truck.'

As it happened, our lioness was more interested in escaping the amorous attentions of the lion who had followed her into the spotlights. She would have none of this mating game, and to prove the point she sat down again.

The gates of the Satara rest camp had closed at dusk, and yet here we were prowling around in the Kruger National Park in the dead of night. This is frowned upon by the authorities, and we were lucky indeed to have been taken into the park at night by one of the guides. Doing the same unaccompanied, one would have run the risk of becoming a tasty morsel. Everybody who has ever been to the game parks of South Africa has an animal story. It is after all South Africa's biggest tourist draw-card, and the main reason why 15 000 Australians go to the dark continent every year.

At the time of writing, South Africa makes sound economic

sense, with the rand worth only half one Australian dollar (usually it is on a par). There is only one direct flight to Johannesburg every week, operated by South African Airways, although Qantas flies to Harare in Zimbabwe and there are connecting flights from there. If you are counting the pennies then a round trip via Europe is much cheaper. You can visit South Africa on your way back to Australia at no extra cost for a round trip fare of $1600.

How is it that a country which has few political and sporting ties with the rest of the world still manages to attract tourists in large numbers? For an answer one has first to look at the uniqueness of its wildlife and its outstanding game parks. There are thirteen main game parks and a number of smaller, privately owned ones. For the tourist who hires a car and spends his time driving through the parks, the rest camps like Satara represent excellent value, with comfortable, well appointed thatched bungalows, shops and all facilities. It is possible to eat your buffalo steak under the stars and listen to the sounds of the animals in the park bedding down for the night.

Round the fire at night, everybody has their own personal animal story. Many of the kiosks have a visitors' book which records not just the visitors' names, but the animals they encountered: 'Saw two hippos and a baby in the creek...Bob Mannheimer, Des Moines, Iowa.' 'Trucks came round bend in the road...hyenas feasting on remains of kudu carcase... Laurie Sidey, Adelaide, South Australia.'

Every tourist suddenly becomes an instant animal expert, and the Kruger does a brisk trade in animal-spotting books. The variety of animals is bewildering—the Kruger alone has more species than any other game park: 130 species of mammal, 48 species of fish and 114 species of reptile. A random selection taken from a census in 1983 showed a population of 8678 elephant, 29 000 buffalo, 95 415 impala and 25 000 zebra.

Some species are more elusive than others. The big cats, for example, tend to rest in the shade during the heat of the day and are not easy to see. You can count yourself lucky to have seen a leopard or a cheetah but giraffes, elephants and antelope are everywhere. To capture them on film, even with a simple camera, is easy, whereas other animals which blend into the dun-coloured bush are not so easy to photograph—a long lens and a good eye are mandatory. It sounds corny, but after a while you do have to pinch yourself and ask: 'Am I really seeing this?'

At the rest camp at Satara, an American matron from Flagstaff, Arizona, was arguing with a friend. 'I told ya, Mirabelle, there *are* no tigers in Africa. I don't care what you say, honey, it was *not* a tiger it was a lion.'

Apart from the game parks, there is much to see in South Africa, and much that will make the Australian tourist feel at home. South Africa's climate is similar to Australia's, although cities like Johannesburg tend to be less humid than Sydney or Brisbane. If the eucalypts seem familiar they should, they were imported from God's Great Sandbank. In exchange, Australia received its jacaranda, which also blooms in profusion all over Jo'burg.

Johannesburg is not South Africa's most beautiful city, but what it lacks in style it makes up for in aggressiveness and business acumen. To the casual visitor it looks like Manhattan, Hong Kong and Sydney rolled into one. No one stands still here for long; if you did you would be trampled in the rush. An office building still standing after twenty years is the exception rather than the rule. It is more likely to have been ripped down to make way for another skyscraper.

Johannesburg wouldn't exist at all if it were not for an Australian prospector called George Harrison, who stumbled across a strange looking rock about 5 kilometres away from where the present city now stands. Harrison didn't know it at the time, but the chunk of rock he held in his hand was part of the only surface outcrop of the main gold bearing reef of the Witwatersrand. Harrison pegged the first claim on the reef and then stumbled off into the bush never to be heard of again; some say he was taken by a lion. Foolishly he sold the claim for £10. Since then, it is a matter of record that many millions of dollars' worth of gold have been taken from Johannesburg's mines.

You can still go underground today, at the Crown Mine near Johannesburg. The descent is undertaken in a well lit cage and not at all claustrophobic. To add to the authenticity, visitors get to wear a miner's lamp and helmet and even gumboots are provided. Unfortunately, they take the gumboots off you again when you get topside. This is a pity, for otherwise you could probably take part in the gumboot dances performed by black mineworkers.

This is the so-called *isicathulo* of the Bhaca tribe. It dates back to a time when a missionary banned the tribe from performing its traditional dance because he considered them to be pagan. Instead, he taught them a more genteel Australian folk dance which the Bhaca perform in Wellington boots as a gesture of protest.

Meeting black Africans in their own environment can be very rewarding. It is worthwhile, for example, to take a tour around the black township of Soweto, outside Johannesburg. You need to obtain a guide and a permit to go there, but these are readily available. More than one million black workers travel into Johannesburg to work every day, returning to Soweto at night. To the casual visitor it is a wilderness of little boxes standing in a sea of broken glass and derelict cars. In fact, as our guide pointed out, the blacks here have a higher standard of living than those in other parts of Africa. Many own their own homes and cars. Soweto has a number of black millionaires, but even they are not allowed to live in the posher suburbs of Johannesburg. Their luxurious homes, with their high security fences, stand out among the rows of identical prefab-style houses. I had hoped to visit a shebeen to drink Kaffir beer with the locals but was advised that this might not be safe. Instead we drove to a grog shop and I tasted the stuff from its cardboard container. It did nothing for me, although it clearly has some applications for grouting bathroom tiles. An enormous black worker with a physique like Viv Richards stood over me in the grog shop and asked where I was from. 'Australia?' he murmured. 'Why don't you play cricket with us any more?'

Sundays in Johannesburg are about as exciting as a bowl of cold rice pudding. The influence of the Dutch Reformed Church is still a powerful one, and pubs, cinemas and many restaurants are closed. Small wonder then that many citizens tend to make good their escape to kick up their heels in Sun City. Sun City is an extraordinary phenomena, a Reno or Las Vegas in the middle of the veldt.

Gambling of all sorts except horse racing is taboo in the Republic of South Africa. Not so in the independent black state of Boputhatswana where roulette, blackjack and poker machines are quite legal. Sun City in Boputhatswana brings the gamblers and pleasure seekers up from Johannesburg in their droves, and they spend big money too. Outside the casino, illuminated by the green spotlights playing on the ornamental fountains, are the rows of Mercedes and Rolls Royces. You can get anything you want in Sun City, from a top line variety show with a name artiste to a soft-core pornographic film. It takes half an hour to get there by plane and many people fly up from Johannesburg just for the night so that they can play the tables.

For my money, Cape Town is the most attractive city in South Africa. Whatever pictures of Table Mountain you may have seen in the tourist brochures, they will not have done the place justice, and a ride to the top in a cable car is a must. Evenings in Cape Town can be fun, especially dining in the town's Malay Quarter. If you are lucky you may be entertained by one of Cape Town's distinctive close harmony vocal groups. In every sense they're a band on the run. The night we dined in the Malay Quarter, a film crew was recording their slow, shuffling progress through the narrow streets of the Malay Quarter, accompanied by drums, trumpets and tambourines.

Cape Town is the starting place for one of the great train journeys of the world—the Blue Train which travels the 1600 kilometres to Pretoria in twenty-six hours. It only has accommodation for 108 passengers so it is necessary to book well in advance to be sure of your seat on this piece of travelling nostalgia. The most spectacular section of the route is through the Cape Mountains and over the Hex River pass which is covered in daylight. Daylight is something of a misnomer. Looking through the window of my carriage I noticed that everything appeared to have a golden hue. The conductor explained that I *was* viewing the world through a thin film of South African gold which is sandwiched between the window glass to keep down the glare from the harsh African sun.

Everything about the Blue Train is up-market. Some carriages contain complete three-bedroom suites with lounge bedroom and bathroom. The food in the dining car is *cordon bleu*, the wine cellar excellent. Our trip on the Blue Train coincided with Australia's winning the America's Cup Yacht Race, and as the train was full of American tourists we celebrated in style. Thus it was that our somewhat seedy group arrived bleary-eyed in Johannesburg the next morning, ready to catch the plane back to Australia.

Jetting around

'REPORTER Involvement' is one of those fancy terms which is supposed to mean putting the reporter into the film story to add a bit of colour. The silliest example of this I remember was when Senator Edward Kennedy got involved in the Chappaquiddick Island affair. To save the lives of the girls who were trapped in a car underwater, Senator Kennedy was supposed to have swum the width of the river. To make his point, the American television news reporter I saw dived into the drink and tried it for himself. I can't say that it added much to the story, except that it got the camera wet.

Working for the ABC's 'Towards 2000' programme I always put myself in line for stories that involved aeroplanes. In 1982 I achieved the doubtful distinction of becoming the first Australian journalist to fly in the new F/A 18 Hornet fighter for the Royal Australian Airforce.

Supersonic flight was not for me a new phenomenon. Years ago, in England, I had elected to fly in one of the RAF's supersonic fighters. People looked glazed with indifference as I described how I had travelled from England to the Norwegian coast in a little over eight minutes. So ten years later here I was in southern California, strapped to five tonnes of screaming aluminium, wondering why I hadn't done as my mother had said and got myself a secure job in banking or insurance.

To fly in the F/A 18, or for that matter any high performance aircraft, you have to wear a G-suit, boots, and a brightly coloured helmet with a visor which makes you look like Darth Vader. The G-suit is a natty neoprene number which straps around your backside and your thighs, and is supposed to stop the blood going where it wants to. And just for the record, when a jetplane is being thrown around the sky, the blood wants to go *all over the place*. In normal manoeuvres, such as tight turns or loops, it wants to go into your legs and you black out, unconscious. A 'red-out' is when the blood rushes into your head (usually in negative G manoeuvres, such as outside loops). The curious thing about the G-suit is that it acts like a constricting corset, stopping the blood from rushing into your legs. When you have been squeezed into all this ridiculous suiting, you are helped into the cockpit and trussed up like a child, while all the time the strapper-in is whispering comforting, words. But even before they would let this 'dumb Limey schmuck' into their 'airplane' there were other hurdles.

They forced me into a decompression chamber and told me to write my name while they simulated taking me up to an altitude of 30 000 feet. There were no noticeable effects apart from the fact that a rubber glove suspended from the ceiling of the chamber swelled up until it looked as if it had elephantiasis. 'That's your lungs', said the instructor, whose name was Chuck. It may have looked like his lungs but I hoped it didn't look anything like mine.

The decompression chamber wasn't so bad. Pure oxygen was good for a hangover, at least. Then, to my horror, the US Navy announced that it was necessary for me to ride the ejection trainer. This quite literally meant having an explosive cartridge detonated under my bottom which would fling me 60 feet into the air. 'You pull the handle between your legs,' said the instructor, 'and whatever you do, don't look down.' I pulled the handle and nothing happened. So I looked down. Just at that precise moment, what appeared to be a thermo-nuclear device kicked me in the backside and I suddenly found myself sitting virtually on the ceiling.

I appeared to have passed the test for next day we lined up on the runway and headed off across the Nevada desert armed with two small blue painted practice bombs and 570 rounds of

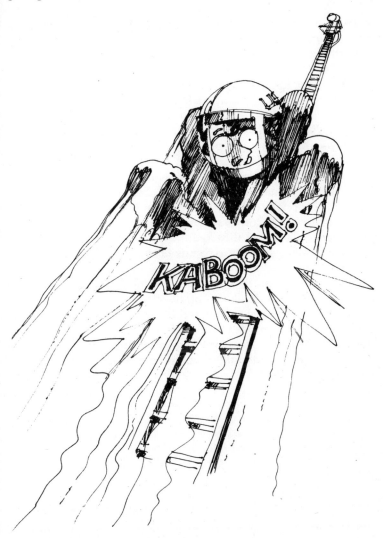

ammunition. To record this adventure I was carrying a small portable movie camera which, because of the G forces, spent most of the time wedged against my chest.

Flying in the F/A 18 is like playing a very sophisticated game of space invaders. In front of the pilot are not conventional instruments, but three television screens which tell the pilot everything he needs to know about the aircraft. As we zoomed down onto an imaginary target and pumped away with the cannon in the nose, a digital read-out told us how many rounds we had expended. I saw a small puff of smoke in the desert as one of the small practice bombs impacted, then before I knew it we were 20 000 up in the sky again. Then we were snaking our way through the contours of a dried-up river bed still doing 800 miles an hour.

'Wow!' said the pilot over headphones. 'Whaddya think, Mr Watson? It's just like sex, isn't it?' I couldn't quite see the analogy, especially as my head was being forced into my shoulders by the G forces and my field of vision was alternately going grey, black and then red.

A week later we saw the results of my in-flight photography. In my terror I had turned the camera on its side so every shot had the horizon at right-angles. But then at least I had not committed the cardinal sin of throwing up into the oxygen mask. 'Where you sick?' enquired the strapper-in as the canopy was opened. 'Er, no not really,' I said. I just hope he never opened the small plastic bag I inadvertently left in the pocket of my flying suit. Wonderfully thoughtful of Kodak to provide sick bags with their film . . .

The great Aussie holiday

Although we often wax lyrical about the pleasures of overseas travel the plain fact is that the vast majority of Australians stay at home for their holidays. I've heard the oft quoted statistic about one million Aussies going overseas every year but the truth of the matter is that a great number of them are business travellers and their fares are paid by their firms. A large proportion of the rest are what the travel industry calls VFR—Visiting Friends and Relatives.

For those who remain in Australia, the vast majority drive interstate in their private cars and stay with relatives. The day after Boxing Day they're all thundering down the Hume Highway in their Chrysler Sigmas and their 200Bs, with their wretched, vomiting children who have names like Bruceen and Wayne, and their awful caravans with names like 'Dunromin' and 'Eureka', and their thin-lipped wives moaning and whingeing because they've been up since half past four making sandwiches and preparing flasks of tea. And in addition to the wife and kids there'll be the mother-in-law and the budgie and the cat and the retarded lavatory brush which could be Bruceen's pet Chihuahua. And they'll have the portable video game, the protable TV set, the portable potty and the hairdryer.

That night you'll find yourselves next to them in the Sunnyholme Caravan Park. Wayne will have been given one of those infuriating, midget-sized motor bikes that make far too much noise for their size, and the old man will show him how to ride it by riding around the caravan park until half past ten at night.

And that night they'll watch the soap operas and learn what's happening in the world from Brian Henderson and Mike Willessee ('On yer, Mike'). The next day, they'll play noisy games of football on the beach and kick sand in everybody's faces. And in the evening they'll all descend on the local RSL. and the wives will drink rums and coke and brandies and dry and the men will drink beer and talk about the fish they're not going to catch, and the women will talk about unspecified uterine problems and children. The children, meanwhile, will be in the corner fighting and crying and vomiting.

The next day the men will be out hosing and polishing their Sigmas just like they do at home. And they'll talk about how they were thinking of going to Noumea for a change but the Frogs are so arrogant and anyway there's going to be a war there. And the kids will still be fighting and vomiting and with any luck Bruceen will tread on a blue ring octopus and have to go to the local base hospital. And the wives will spend the entire fortnight in the caravan talking about the IUD and having their tubes tied, and making baked dinners and not getting suntans and getting progressively more thin-lipped and smoking lots of small cigarettes.

The husbands, meanwhile, will go out in flotillas of small, aluminium boats to catch flathead and catch nothing and drink beer and get drunk instead. And they'll get hooks stuck in their hands and spend the rest of the holiday smothered in mercurochrome.

In evenings they'll sit in their annexes eating one foot steaks covered in blow flies and drinking beer and talking about the bloody abbos and the bloody government and the bloody wife. And the kids will still be fighting and vomiting and the wife will have a headache. And the old man will adjust the tappets on the Sigma with the socket set even though they don't need adjusting. And he'll wish he had stayed at home and gone to the pub with the boys. And on the way home up the Hume he'll get stuck in a seven-mile traffic jam either side of Goulburn.

And he'll say it's the last family holiday ever and the wife will say she wants a divorce. And the old man will say he wants a beer.

And next year, at the same time, they'll do it all over again.

The Bullet

I F the timetable reads that the train will depart at three minutes past noon, then that's exactly when the Bullet train in Japan will leave the station. It is one of the fastest train services in the world and reaches 200 kilometres an hour. For the tourist, possibly the most scenic trip is from Tokyo to Kyoto through the fascinating outskirts of the sprawling capital and then through the Hakone National Park and the distant snowcapped peak of Mt Fuji. From this very modern, almost futuristic train, you will also watch timeless scenes of workers in the rice fields wearing their coolie hats.

Inside the carriages, everything is extremely organised. Hostesses wear white gloves, and wheel trolleys up and down the central aisle selling rice crackers, sweets and Japanese tea.

To travel by rail offers an extended look at the idosyncrasies of the locals and this train is no exception. Soon after the Bullet was introduced in the mid-sixties, Susan Kurosawa, who had only just arrived in the country, and was still in her teens, boarded wide-eyed and very excited. To her amazement, the Japanese men had taken their clothes off and were sitting there wearing nothing but baggy white underwear. Although it is totally acceptable, she found it mind-boggling to be sitting among all these half-naked men. They were mostly businessmen who had removed their expensive suits finding it quite practical and more comfortable to hang them up and make the journey in their underwear.

That wasn't all. In Japan it's a common practice to carry small flasks of cold, green tea to refresh oneself on a journey. Susan's fellow travellers had put these containers on the windowsills of the train. To her, they looked for all the world like little specimen jars, and she was horrified to see they were drinking the contents. Near-naked men, specimen jars? Susan asked herself 'What am I doing here? What *is* going on in this country.'

Travellers please note such practices still occur on Japan's most famous train.

Last tango in Tufi

Tufi in New Guinea has to be the nearest thing in the world to a tropical paradise. Black sand beaches, waving palms, native huts nestling near the waterline. New Guinea is a fabulous country. Fabulously expensive too; the only people who can afford to go there are the Americans who have usually been everywhere else.

We had gone to New Guinea to make a travelogue for the ABC. We groaned inwardly as we saw who our travelling companions were to be—a party of thirteen American matrons, mostly retired schoolteachers. The prospect of tramping around the Central Highlands listening to the voice of Middle America didn't exactly fill us with glee: 'This is cawfee?' 'Hey look at all them artifacts, Doris. We ain't got nothing like that back home in Des Moines.' 'Look at all these funny numbers. Three hundred dollars for a candy bar. I don't believe it!' And so on.

The only member of the party who wasn't 60 in the shade was a rather pneumatic Jewish girl from Brooklyn. Her name was Velma, and Velma was a Jewish-American princess. Velma was carrying at least $1000-worth of the most expensive camera equipment which she kept on dropping in the mud. To have described her as garrulous would have been doing her a grave disservice. She could have talked under the proverbial wet cement. Velma zeroed in on the all male film ensemble like one of New Guinea's celebrated mosquitoes. It wasn't long

before she earned the sobriquet 'Spanner' from the film crew.
'Why do you call her Spanner?' I asked the cameraman.
'Because every time she walks by I feel my nuts tighten,' he said
with a grim smile. During our three weeks' stay in New Guinea,
Velma made it clear that she would be prepared to bestow her
not inconsiderable favours upon anyone. The film crew went
about their work soberly, suppressing the occasional shudder.

We were in fact a day late arriving in Tufi. It was not our
fault, simply the fact that the runway was waterlogged and the
plane couldn't land. But the word of our impending arrival had
gone around the native community. Un be known to us, a huge
crowd of natives had gathered, bedecked in bird of paradise
feathers and ass-grass. They had waited in vain for the television men so that they could perform their traditional sing-
sing. Our names were, appropriately enough, mud. When the
plane finally landed we found the place deserted. Tufi was a
former Methodist Mission station. It was a Sunday. And there
was no hotel, no bar, and nothing to drink. The Tufians did not
seem exactly excited by our appearance. We gathered they were
slightly peeved about our non-arrival. No matter, we persisted.
We would still like to film the sing-sing. Could word be sent to
the outlying villages and the dance group reassembled.

We were not unduly bothered whether the ensemble re-
appeared or not. At any event if they arrived after nightfall we
could do nothing, because there was no mains power and the
generator had broken down. We were, as the Americans say, in
a no-win situation. Miraculously, someone produced a duty free
bottle of Scotch. Night fell, the dance team had not arrived and
there was no chance of any filming. Even some of the American
matrons started to loosen up. In darkness, beyond the circle of
light from the camp fire, Velma licked her lips in anticipation.
She had selected her victim and even now was leading him
down to the black sand beach for a moment of gritty passion.

In the sky, the tropic moon burned only for them. Locked
together on the warm sand they felt completely alone. Or so
they thought. With a hiss a dozen outrigger canoes slid up onto
the beach disgorging warriors bedecked with parrot feathers
and carrying spears. 'Oh, my Gaaard,' shrieked Velma.
Whooping excited cries, the warriors stepped over the prostrate

bodies of the lovers and made their way up the beach to be immortalised on celluloid.

The word had gone out to the far villages. Natives by the score were arriving to put on their best show for the television men. Unfortunately, owing to the duty free Scotch, the camera crew were now insensible. Velma meanwhile, wept warm tears into the black sand. How could she tell the folks back home in Brooklyn that even in volcanic New Guinea, the earth had not moved?

The great wall

IMAGINE flying all the way to China's capital, Beijing, then catching a bus 75 kilometres to the Great Wall and not at least stepping off to walk along this fantastic construction. Mr Thomas, however, simply wasn't interested. After all, he could see the Wall from the shop down the road where warm beer was on sale. Everyone else in the group, both young and old, headed to the point at Badaling where tourists can walk along the Wall. Seen from the ground, the Wall extends to the left and right for about a kilometre and most of our group chose to climb to the left which is a little less steep.

The Great Wall was built more than 2000 years ago, between 476 and 221 BC. China was then made up of seven strong powers and each built its own section at strategic points along their borders. This served to keep the enemy's forces from making any further advances. But in 221 BC, China was unified and the first Emperor of the Chin dynasty linked up the separate walls. That took about ten years and created 6000 kilometres of Great Wall.

At Badaling, the best preserved section of the wall, the climb is reasonably steep but you can lean against the side and absorb the view anywhere. There are some people, of course, who are determined to go as far and as fast as time permits. Two of the fitter fellows, Tony and David, almost ran out of sight for 2 kilometres towards Mongolia. David reported, 'I was surprised at the hawkers selling what they described as ancient Chinese coins. There we were huffing and puffing, with no other tourists in sight, and the locals were trying to palm off coins in what I thought was Communist China.'

Another tourist commented, 'To think this part of the Wall is the only man-made construction that can be seen from space. And I'm standing on it!' And yet another commented, 'The climb's incredibly hard work but it's worth it. You can really *feel* the history. But it must have been a hell of a lot harder for the poor buggers who built it 2000 years ago.'

All in all it was thirsty work at 30°C and even a warm beer, orange or cola sounded more than acceptable, so we scooted past the souvenir stalls to the shop selling drinks. Mr Thomas was standing there sipping on a warm beer and proudly sporting an 'I've climbed The Great Wall' T-Shirt. As the saying goes, 'You can't always believe what you read.'